#Sal...

#SaveOzStories

Geraldine Brooks · Isobelle Carmody
Peter FitzSimons · Richard Flanagan
Jackie French · Anna Funder
Nikki Gemmell · Morris Gleitzman
Kate Grenville · Andy Griffiths
Jane Harper · Chloe Hooper · Toni Jordan
Thomas Keneally · David Malouf
Monica McInerney · Alex Miller
Frank Moorhouse · Matthew Reilly
Michael Robotham · Magda Szubanski
Christos Tsiolkas · Tim Winton

MELBOURNE
UNIVERSITY
PRESS

MELBOURNE UNIVERSITY PRESS
An imprint of Melbourne University Publishing Limited
Level 1/715 Swanston Street, Carlton, Victoria 3053, Australia
mup-info@unimelb.edu.au
www.mup.com.au

First published 2016
Text © individual contributors, 2016
Design and typography © Melbourne University Publishing Limited, 2016

Text design and typesetting by Cannon Typesetting
Cover design by Philip Campbell Design
Printed in Australia by McPherson's Printing Group

National Library of Australia Cataloguing-in-Publication entry

#SaveOzStories/contributors, Richard Flanagan [and 23 others]

9780522870800 (paperback)
9780522870817 (ebook)

Copyright—Australia.
Copyright—Duration—Australia.
Copyright—Government policy—Australia.
Authors, Australian—Legal status, laws, etc.
Book industries and trade—Law and legislation—Australia.

Other Creators/Contributors:
Flanagan, Richard, 1961–

346.940482

Contents

The History

In 2015 the Australian Government requested the Productivity Commission investigate Australia's intellectual property rules. The regulation of the book industry formed part of that review. The Commission's draft report released in 2016 recommended two major changes to the industry. The first recommendation was to abolish parallel importation rules (PIRs) that ensure the Australian market isn't flooded with overseas-published editions. Currently booksellers cannot import bulk copies of books published offshore if an Australian publisher has produced an Australian edition within fourteen days of the original publication overseas. The second recommendation was to reduce the period of copyright protection for published works from the current seventy years after an author's death (or publication, whichever is later) to a mere fifteen to twenty-five years. The first recommendation was endorsed by the Turnbull Government, the second recommendation did not win the government's support. If the current PIRs are abolished, the ramifications for Australian authors, editors, designers, publishers, printers and booksellers are serious. A $2.2 billion industry which is innovative and highly competitive in the global marketplace will be irrevocably damaged. The industry will certainly contract, there will be fewer books published, less diversity and higher prices. Most importantly the Australian book-buying public who have remained enthusiastic consumers of Australian stories will be denied their right to a literary culture that is home-grown, authentically of this place. This book is written by our finest writers. It explains what is at stake and asks for the support of every Australian citizen who has enjoyed reading an Australian story.

Introduction

#SaveOzStories is a gift from the book industry to Australian readers of all ages, in the country and the city, who enjoy browsing in our wonderful bookshops and libraries and who share books with friends and family.

For over four decades Australians have had the pleasure of reading stories about ourselves written by successive generations of original and creative Australian writers. However, it is not by chance that we now have our own literary culture. Once upon a time, publishers sitting in offices in London or New York decided what we read and when. Since the 1970s an ecosystem has developed to ensure Australians read Australian writers. Those writers have been nurtured by modest grants, publishers with an appetite for risk, enthusiastic editors, world-class designers, dedicated local printers and passionate booksellers.

Every industry must confront change, every business needs to be flexible. The book industry is a case study in innovation, from the invention of the printing press in the fifteenth century to books delivered direct to mobile devices in the twenty-first century. The Australian book industry has collectively created a flourishing, authentic literary culture, which proudly tells our stories to readers here and abroad. The invention of a global marketplace has enabled our writers to find international as well as local readers. But this happy circumstance is a direct result of that very specific and local ecosystem that enabled writers to develop and attract readers over a succession of books. Overnight success is the exception, not the rule.

So *#SaveOzStories* invites Australian readers into the experience of our finest writers as they argue in defence of the local book industry. It matters because it is unacceptable for the next generation of children to be deprived of stories in which they can recognise themselves, it matters because writers and writing are fundamental to a civil society, it matters because without a 'fair day's pay for a fair day's work' most writers will be priced out of business and into penury.

There is a curious contradiction at the heart of the current debate about territorial copyright. On the one hand the abolitionists argue that commercially competent businesses will survive, while at the same time arguing that writers as owners of intellectual property should cede their property rights to a 'free' market.

#SaveOzStories offers you the opportunity to think about the value of Australian writers and their stories that we are privileged to enjoy. The book came into being because of a unique collaboration across the whole book industry. Particular thanks go to over twenty of our very finest writers who have donated their intellectual property to create this

book. If you feel convinced by their argument you may want to sign the petition (reproduced at the back of this book) or join the Books Create campaign. Books, in whatever format or device come into being because of human endeavour. Our heartfelt thanks to Michael Leunig, a brilliant cartoonist and friend. His cover is an exquisitely precise expression of the point of a culture of our own. At MUP the meticulous attention of editor Louise Stirling and marketing savvy of Monica Svarc created this book.

Thanks are also due to Penguin Random House CEO Julie Burland, Sales Director Gavin Schwarcz and Publishing Director Ben Ball, HarperCollins CEO James Kellow, Text Publishing Publisher Michael Heyward, Allen & Unwin CEO Robert Gorman, Pan Macmillan CEO Ross Gibb, Hachette Managing Directors Louise Sherwin-Stark and Justin Ractliffe, OpusGroup Executive Chairman and Group CEO Richard Celarc, Griffin Press General Manager Sales Ben Jolly, *Sydney Morning Herald* Editor-in-Chief Darren Goodsir and Editor Judith Whelan, Australian Booksellers Association CEO Joel Becker, over three hundred booksellers across the nation and countless newsagents.

Louise Adler
Chief Executive, Melbourne University Publishing
August 2016

Geraldine Brooks
Own Goal

Well, I did it. I toiled through the 549 pages of the draft report. I'll never get those hours back. I could've been reading a good novel.

Has the little bubble place-marker ever oozed so slowly down the right-hand side of a laptop screen? If so, I can't recall it. It's a rich irony. I just spent an entirely unproductive afternoon reading a Productivity Report.

One thing's for sure: they don't call it the dismal science for nothing. Five hundred and forty-nine pages of economist-speak are enough to strike despair into the heart of someone who loves the English language. Here's a paragraph, plucked at random:

> An effective IP [intellectual property] system is one that seeks to rectify the inherent problems in the supply and use of ideas. It must provide incentives that help to overcome the potential underprovision of ideas that

stem from the public–good nature of knowledge, as well as make sure that the ideas that are generated are disseminated for further innovation to occur. Where it is not possible for the system to correct the under-provision entirely, it should still seek to address the most onerous problems that inhibit the creation and dissemination of new ideas.

If I were to encounter this in a high-school writing class, I'd put a red line right through it. I *think* it says that we want to do the best we can to reward creativity so that more people will be able to get their ideas out there.

Yet the report's recommendations are all about stripping away the rewards of creativity. Let's crewcut the duration of copyright. (Oh, wait—we can't. Other countries are smart enough to recognise that creators deserve to profit from their work for more than fifteen years and we've signed agreements with them.) But here's something no-one else does that we *can* do: irreparable harm to Australian publishing! We can strip the protections that many successful and innovative nations give their own industries, and be one of the few that doesn't have territorial copyright.

That will be okay, says the report, because the government can step in and subsidise Australian writers directly, with grants. Right. That would be the same government that just got done with gutting the Australia Council. And even if Malcolm Turnbull were to be magically invaded by a socialist-leaning body snatcher, what Australian taxpayer would seriously prefer to give their own hard-earned pay to a writer they haven't chosen, rather than proffer a few cents or a dollar extra to buy a book that they actually want?

Australian publishing is a stellar success. The price of books is falling, the number of titles to which Australians enjoy access is rising, and the quality and diversity of Australian writing has never been more breathtaking.

I'm lucky enough to be published all over the world, but nowhere more successfully than in Australia. The design, the marketing and the publicity talent in Australian publishing houses is second to none.

One reason Australian publishing has thrived is the small margin of protection offered by territorial copyright—the same protection enjoyed by publishers in many advanced nations in the world.

Please don't let them end it. No Australian ever cheered an own goal.

Isobelle Carmody

My name is Isobelle Carmody. I am fifty-eight years old. I have written more than thirty books and many short stories. My books have been largely published for children or young adults though I have written for adults, too. I wrote my first book in 1972, when I was fourteen years old. That was *Obernewtyn*, which was published in my twenties. I have been published for over three decades. Everything I have written is still in print. I have written for long enough that many of those who started reading me when I was first published are now mothers and fathers, aunts and uncles, even grandparents, many of whom still read my books and a good many of whom give them and read them to their children and grandchildren.

This is what it is to be a children's author.

There is a remarkable longevity in it because adults who love books as children don't forget these books, as they may forget an adult book they read last year. They cherish the books they read as children and young adults as a part of their childhood, and in time pass them on to their children and share that love with them. Presumably some of the Productivity Commission have children and it may be that they were read to as children, and read to their children. I hope so.

Did you think of the part we played in your childhood and that of your children's childhoods at all when you drafted your recommendations for changes to intellectual property arrangements? Did you think of how your recommendations would affect us and our work, past and future?

The former Treasurer, Mr Hockey, directed you to consider whether current arrangements provided an appropriate balance between access to ideas and products and encouraging innovation and investment and the production of creative works. You were to consider such matters as Australia's trade obligations and the relative contribution of intellectual property to the Australian economy, and you were to recommend changes to the current system that would improve the overall wellbeing of Australian society.

Did it ever trouble you that the copyrights held by authors and illustrators were lumped in with the rights of the holders of industrial patents, trademarks, registered designs, plant breeders' rights and circuit board rights? Did it never strike you that this might not be appropriate, and that your document might say so?

You came up with the two recommendations that I would like to argue against. You recommended that Australia scrap parallel import protections, and in the now infamous clause 4.2 you suggested doing what no signatory to the Berne Convention has done: not just cutting the length of copyright term, but cutting it to *fifteen to twenty-five years* after creation, *not* after my death.

Do you understand that your clause means you are suggesting cutting off my ability to earn from an original piece of work that you did nothing to aid, or promote or produce, and which is my living and the sole support of my partner and daughter, since I am the only breadwinner in my family? It is some relief to know that the government of the day has decided not to accept this particular recommendation.

I do not like to talk about money—we have had a tough few years because I was finishing the last in the seven-book series I began at fourteen, because one fact of being a full-time writer is that when I don't publish, I don't earn. But I have always taken the time I needed to do the best I can despite pressure from readers, my publishers and the people to whom I owe money. Do you understand that by recommending a reduction to the length of time I can own my work, you are effectively forcing me to write an entire series within your timeframe rather than the one that will produce the best creative work? In this way you are directly impacting my creative choices. Your recommendations should reflect that fact.

Do you see how your statement 'the commercial life of most works is less than 5 years' does not fit my work? In fact it does not fit the way in which children's books and books for young adults are published and sell, year after year, generation after generation. Nor does it fit any classic book that continues to sell. Your statement encompasses only airport novels that sell off the front line and then cease to sell. Or books that are not successful commercially for one reason or another. That is not most books. Certainly it is not my books. My books have had a commercial life of three decades, and counting. I would like you to correct your draft to include an acceptance of the damage you will do to me as a writer of books for children and young adults, and suggest the compensation you will pay me for loss of projected income. Your recommendations will not only impact my ability to support my family, but my ability to write—I am a full-time writer. If I cannot earn a living by writing, then I must do so in another way, if indeed that is possible for someone who has spent their life at this one career. If I get a job working at something other than writing, then I will write less, if at all. That does not increase my wellbeing and it might be that the several hundred thousand people who have read my books over two generations would not feel this would improve their wellbeing either. I request that your Productivity Report note the loss of future books I might write.

To use your terminology, if you keep your recommendations as they are, then I wish you to acknowledge the damage you would do to *my productivity*, and I would like to know what it is that Australia will gain by so doing.

In addition, your commission statement says that 'Evidence suggests much of the returns from copyright protected works are earned by intermediaries, rather than authors ...' That may be so, but over my life as a writer, save for the last few years, I have earned a great deal of money. My last six-month royalty cheque was not small. Forty thousand of it was for my backlist, including three books that I would not now own, were your recommendations in place, and year by year, I would lose other work that now earns me a very good living. Will you recommend compensation for those of us who did earn a living from our writing?

It is true that Penguin Books and Allen & Unwin and Ford Street Books and Hachette and Lothian and all of the publishers that have published me over the years and who will publish me in the future, if they survive your recommendations, which means all of the people who work for them, too, have earned a good deal as well. Perhaps more than me collectively. But how is that a problem to the Australian Government or Australian people? Surely that is productivity at work. And how would cutting off my living address that if it is a problem?

I would also like to take issue with the statement in your draft that 'Few, if any, creators are motivated by the promise of financial returns long after death'. I hope that I have made it clear that I have and do make a living out of my writing and I expect to go on doing so, despite the vagaries and ups and downs of the market and a creative life. And because I can make a living as a writer, I can go on writing my books, hopefully until I die. But a good portion of my income and the income of any long-time writer is their backlist. A good writer is a writer with a strong backlist that continues to sell because it supports you while you write. And let me tell you most sincerely that I have seldom met a writer who was not striving to be a full-time writer—to build a backlist that would enable them to write full-time. In fact every writer surely is motivated by the hope that they will be able to make a living from their writing. As to earnings after my death—I have a daughter and the only thing I will be able to leave her is ownership and guardianship of my body of work. Unless this Commission's recommendations ensure I will have nothing of my work to leave her.

Frankly, most writers sacrifice the security of heath care and super and a job with benefits for writing and filling in the gaps by teaching, speaking, editing or doing any part-time job. And your draft report presumes people willing to work for nothing don't *want* payment. It ignores the reality that working for nothing is sometimes a necessary hardship on the road to actually making a living. If your clause 4.2 is taken up, you will end the dream and hope of almost every writer in this country to be a full-time writer. You will make a nonsense of their sacrifices and the sacrifices of their families until now. The Productivity Commission should acknowledge this in its final report.

And what of movies and television series and plays and animations based on my work? Did you consider how your recommendations would impact my right to earn money for work based on my work? Last year I signed a contract to allow the Obernewtyn Chronicles to be turned into a television series. Clause 4.2 ensures that I would not own two of those books. And I chose an Australian–New Zealand company over an American company's offer. I could do that because I own my books. I will have a say about how they are filmed and the script that will be used. And the publisher bought my books because they can be sure of exclusivity. I can guarantee that because I own my books. I can ensure they do not become violent or pornographic or ridiculous, or abridged or accompanied by offensive images, because *I own my work.* If your recommendations are to be made, then I want you to include details about how you will protect my work from exploitation.

You might wonder why I have spent so much time on clause 4.2 when it appears you may set that aside. That it is still part of the draft requires that it be addressed thoroughly. It is also the product of the same mindset that produced the recommendation to set aside PIRs.

I wonder, as no doubt many other writers have wondered, why you would suggest setting aside those restrictions, giving an advantage to the dominant US and UK publishing markets which they would certainly not give to us. They are not about to set aside their parallel import restrictions, so why would we? Especially, why would we when we have seen the impact exactly this action has had on the New Zealand publishing industry? I toured both islands last year. Book prices have not gone down and the local publishing industry languishes. I've since used social media and direct contact to ascertain that my impressions were correct. Since the abandonment of PIRs, there are less NZ publishers, less books by local authors being published and sold, and books are not cheaper. At least they are but only because books everywhere are selling at less today than they were in 2006.

As for books being cheaper following the abandonment of PIRs, people have always been able to import cheaper books, or to request that bookshops do so on their behalf, which enables a bookshop to bring in more than one at a time. Bookshops make use of this all the time here.

I was not born with a silver spoon in my mouth. I was the eldest of eight kids, the eldest daughter of a working-class accountant, and his uneducated wife. I knew nothing about publishing when I started to write. I wrote for myself—for solace, for comfort, for love of words and most of all in order to think. My dad died in a car crash when I was fourteen and my mother brought us all up with desperation, optimism and hope, on a widow's pension. I was the first of my family to go to university. Following university I began work as a journalist. Not long after becoming a journalist, I sent my first book off to be published. I did not have an agent. I did not even know such a thing existed. I looked inside the front cover of books I had read and liked, and found the addresses of the publishers in small print. Australian publishers' addresses. I made a list of them. My book was accepted by the first publisher I sent it to. I have never had anything rejected. Penguin published *Obernewtyn*, which was short-listed for children's book of the year. So was its sequel, *The Farseekers*, which also won two other awards. Other of my books have been shortlisted for various prizes. I have twice won book of the year here. This year I was voted Australia's favorite author in a Booktopia popular vote.

I have no doubt this last one was merely the result of overwhelming relief at the fact that I had finally finished the seventh and last book in the series I began writing at fourteen. But I mention all of this not to admire my own career, but as the background for a few salient points.

I am an Australian author, and my voice is an Australian voice. I do not write books with gum trees and kookaburras in them, but nevertheless my stories are firmly rooted in this soil. I have been published overseas but never to the acclaim I have found here. I have been published overseas in translation and in Britain and the US, those great protec-torates of their own literature, but while I did well enough, I have always found my greatest audience here. I have no doubt that, had I been forced to send my books to those overseas addresses I found in books, when I was trying to decide where to send my first book thirty years ago, because there was no local publishing industry, I would not have been accepted.

The UK and US only took me on because of how successful my books were here. Because what I have to say with my stories belongs most truly to my own country. The more I have travelled overseas, the more deeply I have understood that.

Simply put, your proposal to drop PIRs would have ensured that a writer like me was not published here. What publisher would take a risk on such an author unless they were part of a robust industry? Your recommendations will diminish the Australian publishing industry. That is an industry, particularly as far as children's and young adult books go, which is the envy of the English-speaking publishing world. Ours is a thriving, robust industry which as well as earning writers a living, sees vigorous cultural exchange between writers, schools, libraries and the community. We need to tell our stories and we need to hear them in order to grow and change and evolve. I am part of that industry. I am a full-time writer. I make a living out of my writing and I wish to go on doing so. I want to be able to protect my work and pass on the fruit of my labour, untarnished, to my daughter.

A statement read at a public hearing of the Productivity Commission, June 2016

Peter FitzSimons

I tell Australian stories as a significant part of my living. Over the last twenty years or so, I have particularly enjoyed telling in my own fashion such sagas as the *Batavia*, Gallipoli, Kokoda, Tobruk, Ned Kelly, the Eureka Stockade, Nancy Wake, and have just finished—thanks for asking—a book on Villers-Bretonneux. Those books are bought predominantly by Australian families and though my passion is such storytelling, and I am handsomely rewarded for it, it is worth noting here that the whole exercise helps employ as many as five researchers at one time, a whole bevy of editors and publishing people and many others involved in the Australian book industry.

And, of course, I am one of thousands making my living in such fashion. Among them are the likes of Judy Nunn, Nikki Gemmell and Magda Szubanski, while Jimmy Barnes sings those stories and has been busy writing them for a book coming out before Chrissie.

On a Thursday evening recently, we, with other authors, met in the offices of HarperCollins with a variety of publishers and lawyers to look at the government proposals to change the territorial copyright laws by following the Productivity Commission's recommendation to abolish parallel import rules and even bring down the term of copyright from the current seventy years after death to as little as fifteen years.

It is, I grant you, a complex issue, but the bottom line is this: it is our united view—and the view of most Australian storytellers—that beyond all matters of commerce, it is the *duty* of the federal government—of whichever stripe, for now and forevermore—to support the Australian campfire where Australian stories are told, to Australians.

On that evening no-one in the room had any doubt that following the Productivity Commission's recommendations will mean seeing our stores flooded with more and more American and British books, and remaindered editions of our own books, sourced from overseas.

And yes, you're right, all of the aforementioned authors are well established in our trades, and will be fine no matter how the rules change. But Jimmy Barnes was most eloquent in talking about how it worked in the music world, when after they lost the battle on parallel imports back in the nineties, young Australian singers and bands struggled to get the crucial support they needed from the record companies, who are, evermore, only prepared to back established 'brands', not fork out money in the hope that new talent will come through.

Bottom line? Whatever the commercial powerhouses are saying about the virtues of following those recommendations,

it will see the rising damp of Coca-colonisation on our culture rise ever faster to eat away at our own national fabric.
This meeting was not in favour of the proposals.

And I am happy to say, when I put much of the above in
my column in *The Sun-Herald*, it seemed to me that huge
numbers of Australians agreed with me.

Richard Flanagan

It may seem at the moment that the only thing that will save the Australian book industry is moving every publisher and writer into Christopher Pyne's electorate, and making them all wear hi-vis jackets and safety helmets.

For we have in recent weeks discovered that the Turnbull Government is considering proposals for a writer to not have any rights in their work fifteen to twenty-five years after it's first published. So Mem Fox has no rights in *Possum Magic*. Stephanie Alexander has no rights in *The Cook's Companion*. Elizabeth Harrower has no rights in *The Watch Tower*. John Coetzee has no rights in his Booker-winning *Life and Times of Michael K*. Nor Peter Carey to *True History of the Kelly Gang*, nor Tim Winton to *Cloudstreet*. Anyone can make money from these books except the one who wrote it.

The Abbott and now Turnbull Government's record drips with a contempt for writers and writing that leaves me in despair. They want to thieve our past work, and, by ending parallel importation restrictions and territorial copyright, destroy any future for Australian writers.

That contempt has been made concrete in the report of the Orwellian-titled Productivity Commission. The Productivity Commission doesn't dare call books books. Instead they are called—in a flourish not unworthy of Don DeLillo—*cultural externalities*.

In their perverted world view, the book industry's very success is a key argument in their need to destroy the book industry, and *this determination to destroy an industry* is revealed in their report as the real aim of these proposals.

Just one highly revealing quote from the Productivity Commission:

> The expansion of the book production industries over recent decades has attracted and held productive resources, notably skilled labour and capital, that have thereby been unavailable for use in other industries. The upshot will have been reduced growth in employment and output in other parts of the economy.

Replace the clumsy phrase '*book production industries*' with the word '*kulak*', and you would have ideological cant worthy of Stalin.

What they are saying is that without the book industry—which is nothing more than a parasite—the economy would be doing far better. We could all be helping the economy doing real work like, well, being unpaid interns for merchant bankers.

The report's proposals, which even before seeing them the Turnbull Government agreed to endorse, effectively extinguish the Australian book industry as we know it and deliver our market to American and British publishers.

And that's what this government thinks of everyone in this room. Be under no illusion: they want to destroy this industry. And with it, Australian literature. They want you out of a job, they want us no longer writing. Cultural externalities are, after all, external to who and what we are.

And perhaps this is all not so surprising, because the Turnbull Government's decision is not based in reality. Vassals of an outdated ideology unrelated to the real world, they can, when questioned on this issue, only mumble neoliberal mantras that have delivered the world economic stagnation, rising inequality and global environmental crisis. Hollow men, stuffed men, their words rats' feet over broken glass. The only thing these people read are the Panama Papers to see if their own name has cropped up.

This decision to destroy the book industry by removing parallel import restrictions is consistent with the government's relentless assaults on science and scientists. It is of a piece with its ongoing attacks on thought and debate. Who benefits from ignorance and silence other than the most powerful and the richest?

The democracy of thought and discussion that books make possible, the possibility of empathy that books are known to engender, the sense of a shared humanity and the transcendent possibilities that books give rise to, all will be diminished by this profound attack on Australian writing. And we will have returned to being what we were fifty years ago: a colony of the mind.

You have to ask if, at heart, this is not profoundly political, because the disenfranchisement of the imagination is ever the disempowerment of the individual. There is, after all, both a bitter irony and a profound connection in a government that would condemn the wretched of the earth as illiterate, while hard at work to rob its own people of their culture of words.

I had long hoped for bipartisan support for the arts. I have lobbied politicians of all stripes on that basis. I wrote to then prime minister Abbott on this matter. But the last two Liberal governments have been the worst in our history in their treatment of artists and writers.

With their gutting of the Australia Council, with their theft of money for a Book Council that never happened and the money for it vanished into general revenue, they have shown that they do not care, and now, far worse, that they wish to destroy the possibility of a future Australian literature by destroying territorial copyright.

Where is Prime Minister Turnbull's much-vaunted innovative economy in this decision? Where exactly, Prime Minister, are the jobs and innovation in destroying jobs and innovation? We employ people, some 25 000 by last count. We make billions, we pay tax, we make things and we sell them here and we sell them around the world. And all at no cost to the taxpayer. And now Prime Minister Turnbull would destroy it all.

We are not a subsidised industry. The fossil fuel industry gets $18 billion of subsidies. A single South Australian submarine worker gets $17.9 million. And writers? The total direct subsidy for *all* Australian writers is just $2.4 million. That's it. And that's all.

What I say next, I say with heavy heart and only after the deepest thought, because I don't believe in any party. I speak now only for myself.

Fuck them.

This is a government that has no respect for us and no respect for what we do. This is a government that despises books and views with hostility the civilisation they represent. Perhaps it hopes in a growing silence that it might prosper. Certainly, it cares only about one thing: power.

And only on those terms will it listen.

For that reason, if you care at all about books, don't vote Liberal at this election. If you care at all about what books mean, don't vote Liberal. If you value how books can enrich lives, don't vote Liberal. If you think Australian books matter to an Australian society, don't vote Liberal.

Because this is the party of philistines who punish the creators, destroy all that has been created and create nothing but destruction. They should stand condemned for what they have done. To the minister I say, if you have a shred of dignity, resign. His shame, and Prime Minister Turnbull's shame, should be public, well known and long, long, long lived.

For we inside this room and the many, many more beyond it have made something special and unique that helps us become a better people, and which brings our people honour around the world.

This government, which again, and again, has brought Australia only global shame with its follies of cowardice and cruelty has no right now to destroy such a good in our nation as this: the voice of our experience, the words of our people, the tongue of our hope—*our* culture of writing.

In this time of fracture we need more than ever the things that can bring us together as a people, not fear, not the resentments of the many, carefully cultivated to cloak the privilege of the few, but the hope of a society that might discover in books the liberating possibility of a shared humanity. Of a better future. Together.

We need to fight for it. We must not give up. And, if we hold together, I promise you—we shall prevail.

A speech given at the Australian Book Industry Awards, Sydney, 19 May 2016

Jackie French
The People of the Books

When I was a child I knew where Paradise lived. It was in Barker's Bookstore, Brisbane's only bookshop, where I found my lifelong friend, *The Magic Pudding*, and discovered who I was, and what my country may be.

As a child, my world was shaped as Dad read me Thomas Keneally. Half a century later, following the release of Keneally's latest book, the phone rang: 'Hey Jacq, it's Dad. Have you read Keneally's latest?' Deep into his eighties, Dad's voice resonated down the phone as he read me yet another chapter.

Birthdays meant wrapped editions of Judith Wright's poems, Mary Grant Bruce novels, Patrick White or David Malouf: all pre-read. Our family never gives a book until we have read it first.

We are the people of the books: you and I, writers, publishers, booksellers and book lovers, all who love the scent of a new page or the scribbled margin notes on an old one, the pensioner who seeks a cherished companion from her bookshelf, the boy who hunts Australian megafauna in his school library.

I am a reader with a 'three book a day' habit. I am a children's author from passion, and conviction.

I write for kids because each book builds kids' intelligence, creating tools to build the future they imagine. If we wish our children to know their country, its problems and deep potential, we must give them Australian books: classic Australian titles that are kept in print by an Australian book industry, and new titles relevant to our current issues and our society.

I write for kids because for a short while they become each character in every book they read, and when they have finished, they have grown in empathy and understanding. If we want adults with the insight to bridge the divisions in our nation, our young people need Australian books.

I write for kids to show them not what they might want to be when they grow up, but to help them find the question 'How do I want to live?'

I write about Australia's history, so our young people will learn not just how we came to be the way we are, but also that the world *will* change—and that if we care enough, we can make sure those changes are good. Every generation of humanity faced challenges, and survived. Humans are good at challenges. What we are not good at is boredom.

I write for kids to show them how to not be bored. I write books that troubled kids can identify with and libraries and literacy programs are cheaper than youth detention centres, drug rehabilitation, prisons and repairing vandalism.

I write for kids because the best way to inspire them to fight for a good future for our species, our country and our world, is to help them love it—and the things in it—from wombats to the stars. If we want an Australian industry that profitably mines asteroids in thirty years' time, give kids books. Creativity is contagious. You catch it from books. It's muscle building for the brain.

Yet would any of these deeply Australian books be published overseas without the security of initial Australian sales to defray the costs, in an Australia that has parallel importation restrictions (PIRs) ripped away? Not if the collapse of the publishing industry in New Zealand after they removed their PIRs is any guide, nor the devastation of the Canadian education publishing industry with their US-style 'fair use' changes. We know what happens. The evidence is there.

Books change lives. They also inspire economic value.

When a child in China, Texas or Korea is raised on *Diary of a Wombat*, they breathe in Australia too, subtly and irrevocably. They then have a context in which to see its potential as future tourists or, in a far larger capacity, as investors. Give me a child at an impressionable age, and I'll give you an investor in twenty years' time.

No trade delegation, no matter how large its budget, can give you the international PR of *Possum Magic* or *The 26-Storey Treehouse*. Plus the Australian economy receives millions of export dollars now, every year for each of those titles, with sales growing, not decreasing, every year.

Australian publishing does not tempt then disappoint with 'boom and bust' export income, as with the mining industry, nor is it heavily subsidised, like manufacturing.

Possibly uniquely for an industry of its size, Australian publishing receives no subsidies at all. It is reliable, sustainable and continually expanding—as long as the Productivity Commission's recommendations are filed forever where they deserve to be, under 's' for 'silverfish'.

That's it, in a nutshell: our government just needs to do nothing on this issue, and the industry's contribution to our culture and economy will continue, growing ever larger, every year.

Seventy years ago Australia's wealth came from sheep, wheat and our manufacturing industries: we made everything from ships and tractors to trains, washing lines, cameras and boots that were then exported across the world. Ten years ago Australia drew its wealth primarily from what was dug out of the ground. Today and tomorrow, wealth and jobs come from ideas: intellectual property.

Which makes it difficult to fathom why the 'Unproductivity' Commission wishes to reduce the intellectual property protected by copyright to as little as fifteen years, claiming that 'few writers write for money'.

Actually, we don't. But we must eat, too.

An Australian can build a house, keep it for their lifetime and pass it on, generation after generation. Why should intellectual property—ideas and creations—be treated differently than physical fabrications? Would the Commissioners seriously suggest that a factory become public property fifteen years after it was built? That a house may be owned for only fifteen years, and can then be taken by whoever grabs it? Why should work that takes me years to research and create be stolen from me?

'Theft' is the accurate word here. What moral reason can be given for stealing my life's work? What economic argument can validate it? Legally these copyright proposals fly in the face of international law. Why did the Commission waste time on an issue that is already protected? How can we take their other recommendations seriously?

This Commission will throw out PIRs with the false promise that it will make imported books cheaper, and more books available to the consumer. If that were the case, why are books now, on average, more expensive in New Zealand than they are in Australia? Where is their data and modelling?

Possibly their myth is based on out-of-date figures. Ten years ago books sold in Australia *were* generally more expensive than the same books sold in the United Kingdom or the United States, but initiatives undertaken by the publishing industry since 2009, together with changing market forces such as online retailing, mean this is no longer the case.

Trust me: with a 'three book a day' habit, I know where book bargains lie. If you doubt, compare prices yourself. Remember to allow for exchange rates and postage.

Easier access and more choice of books? Australians can already order online any books they wish to read from overseas retailers—except the many Australian titles overseas retailers have no wish to stock.

These are the titles that will no longer be published if PIRs are slashed. This means *less* choice in Australia, not more. All other major nations, such as the United Kingdom and the United States, have their own form of PIR, and intend to keep it. Australia needs a level playing field for our $2.2 billion per annum industry to survive.

I am perhaps of the first generation of Australian authors to have Australian books as my childhood mentors and companions. I never dreamed that in my sixties I would need to fight for the existence of an Australian literature industry. That was a battle won by my parents and grand-parents, in the days when an aspiring author had to move overseas. Should I advise the young writers I mentor now to relocate to Ireland, where the government so values writing's contribution to the Irish economy that authors do not pay income tax?

Unlike the Irish Government, the Productivity Commission states that the Australian publishing industry is now *too* successful and so steals skilled workers from more-productive industries.

Yes, the Commission really did say that. No, I don't think they were joking. Should we weep with laughter, or with shame?

Economic rationalism? These conclusions are neither economic nor rational. And yet the supporters of these proposals argue that we sentimental authors have been manipulated to argue for the industry that is our lives, our passion and our blood.

Easy to manipulate? Herding wombats is easier than getting writers to agree, which is what makes panels at literary festivals across Australia so interesting. Pen a pod of poets, and count the daggers. If there were a collective noun for writers it might be 'an argument of authors'.

This is the rarely acknowledged truth: to be a successful writer you must have a mind of vast and quirky strength that can assimilate, analyse and correlate torrents of data into a single document; and a sometimes wicked intellect.

Are we infallible? No.

Are we well equipped to analyse and predict financial and social consequences? Yes. (We can even give a pretense of modesty, especially on the night someone else wins the award.)

When authors with such divergent outlooks as Peter FitzSimons and Thomas Keneally agree on an issue, it is reasonable to assume that they are right.

We are the people of the books. Our words matter, because we see Australia clearly, even if—or especially because—what each of us sees is different.

I am an old woman who has given her life to books. I assumed my books would continue to support my husband and myself. I trusted our government to leave a flourishing and diverse industry to expand, even if that government, collectively, had little interest in the deep cultural gifts our books bring.

Was I wrong?

I challenge Malcolm Turnbull and Bill Shorten. I challenge every politician. Do *you* have the courage to stand with the people of the books? Or do you side instead with those who think a book is only words, that new ideas are to be feared, and do not count even the dollars lost as you rip our industry away? Do you accept we need a clever country to have a strong economy?

Prime Minister: will you be our book thief? Or will you offer us the economic certainty of intellectual copyright to develop the ideas and innovation to drive a strong new economy?

Sixty years ago I'd have kicked anyone who tried to destroy Barker's Bookstore. Today my weapons are only words.

Only words? Why are you reading this if they are 'only words'?

Words are humanity's most powerful weapon. And so I plead with you to use them: to tweet, use Facebook, write to newspapers, to politicians. Demand that those who try to undermine our industry substantiate their claims, explain why what has occurred in New Zealand and Canada will not happen here, attempt to demonstrate why the United States and the United Kingdom and all other major nations are mistaken when they keep their own versions of PIR.

Our books—fiction, history or scientific, books to laugh with, or escape to—are our homeland.

We are the people of the books. Let's keep that paradise alive, the one I found so long ago, in Barker's Bookstore, the one we all must fight for—that myriad of worlds and words and possibilities, Australian books.

Anna Funder

We are gathered here today to celebrate the life of Australian literature.

The Miles Franklin Literary Award is Australia's most prestigious literary prize. Even as a child I knew that the books which got the gold stickers joined a pantheon of the gods of literature: Patrick White, Jessica Anderson, Tim Winton and others. These books tapped into something profound about both humanity and this country. This prize recognises the noble art of making a beautiful world out of language, a world that shows us things about life which are wonderful or terrible or funny, and which life itself can't tell us. A world that shows us who we are.

Though I was far away when my book *All That I Am* won in 2012, I felt that the love I have for my country had been somehow, mysteriously, reciprocated. Writers, too, have a home team, and our home team is our nation. I have toured in many countries, and they all have writers of their own whom they honour and enjoy, who reflect the nation back to itself, from the inside.

We are, all of us, of a nation, in the same way that we are of our parents: inevitably, eternally, in DNA and psyche, shaped by both.

Miles Franklin said: 'Without an indigenous literature, people can remain alien in their own soil.'

Without writers, our inner lives, as well as the inner life of the nation, would remain alien to us. We would not know who we had come from and we would not know who we are. Much as Watson and Crick discovered the helix inside us, writers reveal our cultural, our national, DNA.

Miles Franklin herself scrimped and saved to give this money to good Australian writers 'so as to advance and improve Australian literature'. She had to save hard, because she received only a small export royalty from her British publisher for books sold in her own country.

Miles was living in an era when it was felt that Australian literature could be 'advanced' and 'improved'. This would not have been said about the literature of England, which was allowed just to be, in the full expectation that every generation would throw up a crop of talented, and occasionally truly gifted, writers. We have come a long way from the day when we needed 'advancing' or 'improving'. There are many writers at work in Australia, many very good ones. Australian literature is 'advanced', it is sophisticated and globally celebrated.

It may also be doomed.

People ask me which is easier to write, non-fiction or fiction. Sometimes the question is whether I am ever tempted to tweak reality to produce a better story. The answer is: never. Reality, looked at closely, far outstrips what is credible in fiction. To take a current, dystopian example: the government is considering a proposal from its Productivity Commission that would decimate Australian publishing by allowing overseas publishers to flood the market with their works, and their editions of Australian writers' works—the so-called parallel imports. Let me tell you what this means, with reference to two of my books.

Stasiland and *All That I Am* are published in twenty countries around the world, including several English-language ones. If the government's proposal is adopted, Australian booksellers would be legally able to import editions of these books from the United States, the United Kingdom, Canada, or wherever. For those imports, I would receive what is known as an export royalty. This is much lower than the domestic royalty, which itself, at best, amounts to just over $2 a book. Most often, because overseas publishers are allowed to calculate a royalty after all their costs have been taken out, writers receive nothing at all for these imports.

This means that for my next book, which will likely be published overseas as well as here, my Australian publisher will be unable to offer me an advance of any decent amount because they will know the domestic market has been destroyed and they will not recoup their outlay. This in turn means that I will have to publish first overseas, most likely in the United Kingdom, and a UK publisher will make money instead of an Australian one. This is a disaster for me, for my publisher, and for readers. It means Australia is once more a colony, exporting but not profiting from our own product.

I am now asking myself whether I really want to—indeed can—write a book primarily for a UK publisher. And do they really want the book about Australia I am currently working on? A book which is close to my heart and which, rather ironically it seems now, investigates where our sense of fair play comes from. Perhaps I will not be able to write about my own country and make enough to live on.

Another proposal has been floated by the Productivity Commission: to gut the copyright of authors. This would be to take away my ownership of my work after just fifteen years. Copyright currently endures for my lifetime plus seventy years, for my children and theirs. The Commission's proposal would mean that *Stasiland*, a book which won the most prestigious prize for non-fiction in the world, a book which is studied in universities and schools in many countries, would from *next year* no longer be mine, nor a property for my children. Educational institutions, film-makers and publishers in any country could just use and reproduce it however they liked and not pay me a cent.

If I borrowed money to buy land and build a block of apartments, I would expect to own them until I sold them, to get a return from rent, and to be able, if I wished, to bequeath them to my children. I would expect my risk, work and intelligence to be rewarded. I would not expect the government to expropriate my property at the end of fifteen years. If this copyright proposal seems like a proposal for theft to you, that is because it is. I borrowed money and took a personal and financial risk over many years and I built a world of words, for everyone to enjoy. Now, the Productivity Commission is seriously proposing to expropriate it from me and my family, for no just recompense. This proposal is in fact so bizarre, and would be so damaging to creativity and innovation, that it is beyond the pale of international law. Treaties covering international intellectual property prohibit Australia, for the moment, from making such outrageous changes. The government has wisely recognised this and dropped it. But it is very important for us to have a clear understanding of the kinds of damaging policy recommendations that the Productivity Commission is proposing.

It is important to tell a story from as many points of view as possible. In *Stasiland* I worked hard to understand the points of view of some fairly unsympathetic people, the Stasi men. I work hard to understand monsters, and monstrous things, because I want to write works not only of beauty, but also of witness and of warning. Witness and warning are necessary now, because reality beggars belief. It feels like my country, or at least its government, hates me and all my kind. It feels like our leaders do not want people to see themselves or their country in the variety of ways that literature allows.

This is the forced closure of the Australian mind. It is a fire sale of our intellectual property and our national pride. So, who benefits? The only argument that seems to have been put is that book prices will be cheaper.

There is absolutely no evidence that this is true.

And a $2.2 billion industry which takes no subsidy, makes money, pays tax and employs 25 000 people will be destroyed. To say nothing of the national culture.

Markets, as any economist will tell you, are created. Sometimes this requires legislation, sometimes choices are made to subsidise them. The Australian Government subsidises many markets: car manufacture for years; submarines (each submarine worker is subsidised to the tune of more than

$17 million *each* year); and now some $580 million in proposed subsidies to the milk industry. The banking industry benefits to the tune of some $4 billion because of government regulation and guarantee. There are myriad other examples. Why would the government be seeking to destroy an industry that is completely unsubsidised? An industry that is profitable and flourishing? Certainly publishers, economists and others in the United Kingdom and the United States are looking on in horrified bewilderment.

What we have here is 'economic rationalists' behaving irrationally, seeking to close down a profitable industry and so diminish economic productivity in our country. There are industries where 'global competition' may benefit the consumer: book publishing is not one of them. Neither publishing houses, booksellers nor consumers stand to benefit. I would argue that 'global competition' is better served when we have a national literature which can produce writers of a calibre to win global prizes and then global markets.

As I said, the closer you look, the more reality is not credible. It is possible that these reasons, which make neither economic nor cultural sense, are all there is. But we must keep asking the question, in case the answers, and the effects of the proposed changes, are not clear even to those who are making these changes.

So: who would benefit from the flooding of our market with cheap overseas content? And who would benefit from the erosion of copyright for Australian creators?

The only beneficiaries of the proposed change to parallel imports are overseas publishers. Meanwhile, Australian writers and a democratic Australian culture will be further impoverished.

The only beneficiary of the proposed copyright change is the Googlesphere, to which would be delivered 'free' content—that is to say, my and all other Australian authors' expropriated property. Google's business model requires 'free' (i.e. stolen, or unpaid for) content to be made available so that it can sell ads. Manufacturers such as Apple would also like this 'free' content to sell with their devices. It seems extraordinary that a government-funded commission could seriously propose legislating to allow this theft. Legislating to hand over our cultural property to the Googlesphere for free, and so discourage future Australian innovators from creating anything. And we need to ask, of course, what will, or does, Google and the tech companies give back to the government in return? These are questions which must be explored elsewhere, by people more qualified than I.

But what I can tell you is this. We live in a fast age. We have information at our fingertips, the apparent answers to all the questions of the universe, of history, of local navigation in our computers available at a click. I am all in favour of this new, instant world. But the Googlesphere is also a world of spinning, unattributed facts and factoids, a world without authors, a humming hive of unsourced information and unseen, controlling algorithms. I found this out, rather hilariously, when I was barred from correcting the Wikipedia entry on my own life—what authority did I have? Not enough, apparently.

This is a world in which almost every aspect of your person—from your blood pressure to your book choices, your keystrokes, the sites you visit, your email, where you eat and where you sleep—can be known. Eric Schmidt of Google says: 'We don't need you to type at all. We know where you are. We know where you've been. We can more or less know what you're thinking about.' Google claims this tracking is done so that every time you do a search, what you already want will instantly come back to you. Here is the world made smaller, just for you.

This is also a world in which the governing trope is the selfie. Narcissus sends out pictures of himself, 'liking' others only so as to be 'liked' back. This is a fatal world of mirrors, disguised in the language of consumer choice.

Literature is the opposite of this selfie world, because in literature your self is not reflected back to you. Instead, you see yourself in *others*. This is the basis of compassion, and it works, rather magically, to expand your inner universe. Rather than being tailored to what you already 'like', literature might take you, excitingly, into realms you never knew you needed.

Now, and even more in the future, we need to read books written by independent authors published by Australian publishers. We need to read our way out of the hive.

This is a clever country, a country that has earned its identity, and its self-knowledge, in no small part due to its writers. Let's not outsource our minds to the narcissism of the global algorithm. Instead, let us celebrate the creativity, innovation and brilliance of Australian authors. We wish them long and happy and financially viable careers doing the vital work of making ourselves known to ourselves and the world.

We celebrate by holding up our mirror—all our disparate mirrors—not to ourselves but to this world; to its beauty, its mysteries, its cruelties:

To babies who besot us and one-armed bandits who fleece us;

To fat mining magnates and rotating prime ministers;

To floor-crossers and cross-dressers;

To Papuan High Court justice;

To photographers and pornographers;

To street people and shock jocks;

To footballers—and bogan billionaires;

To stolen children and newly discovered planets;

To Pygmy people and human mules;

To Chinese Government curriculum in NSW schools;

To cloud-seeding, to coke-snorting racehorses;

To islands drowning and children being born;

To being left, to being found;

To stopping time.

Writing is work of ingenious empathy. It is work of compassion as holy as any we are likely to find. We can't afford *not* to have it, or we won't know who we are.

A revised speech delivered on the announcement of the Miles Franklin Shortlist, at the Australian Booksellers Association Conference, 29 May 2016

Nikki Gemmell

I write this in anguish. At the debasement of writers in this country. This is the most despairing time to be an Australian writer for as long as I can remember. Our Prime Minister, Malcolm Turnbull, declared that an Australia of the future has to be agile, innovative and creative; and by his cosmopolitan nature once gave the nation's artistic community hope that he would oversee a great flowering of the arts in the way a Whitlam did, or a Keating. We mistakenly assumed Mr Turnbull took pride in the worlds of artistic creativity and would nurture them as the mark of a mature and dynamic nation. That he would want the arts to flourish under his stewardship, to create a legacy of vision, daring and confidence.

Yet this era is shaping up to be the one where Australia's literary culture is decimated. Where the local publishing industry is torn apart. Where we take an enormous step backwards into a world of Australian letters that sees over-seas publishers as our masters once again—and dismissive ones at that. Where Australian writers are dictated to by publishers in London or New York who are not interested in the nuances of our very particular Australian culture. Because they're just too far away, and they don't care enough. But Australian writers do. As do their readers. Passionately.

Few people, apart from writers themselves, realise how bleak the Australian literary landscape has become. None of us likes to talk about it beyond ourselves. It feels like an admission of failure, of just how ridiculously hard it's become to earn a living from our laptops and pens. With a proliferation of online media outlets and blogs, and a shrinking newspaper market, writers are expected to work for little or nothing now. It feels like we're scrabbling for bones. Editors tell us they don't have the budgets they used to; their markets are shrinking; people don't read like they used to. They expect us to be grateful for the one thing they can throw at us in lieu of a living wage—exposure. For most of us, that does not help put food on the table for our families. The average writer's income in Australia has dropped from $22 000 a year in the past decade to just over $12 900. What other industry has seen such a plunge in wages, and in such relative silence?

Market forces have dictated it. Cheaper e-books have cut into publishers' profits. Bold new players in the booksell-ing industry—the big chain stores like Big W, Target and Kmart—also offer cheaper books, which means squeezing margins all around. Australia Council grants to individual authors have been cut, alongside subsidies for our finest literary magazines. Some, tragically, will fold. Within this climate, statistics show us that adults are reading less. Publishers are reducing print runs, and the author advances that were on offer a decade ago are a distant memory. With all these forces bearing down on local publishers, they're becoming increasingly risk averse—taking punts on fewer titles, and fewer first-time authors.

Some novelist mates—bold, innovative writers—haven't had a publisher in a decade; they've given up. Great writers who've added to the cultural enrichment of this nation but are deemed too non-commercial, in this cautious climate. It's heartbreaking to see writers who've had one or two books published unable to get a book deal now. When Joan London won the Nita B Kibble Prize last year, which recognises the work of an established female writer, she commented, 'I'll just be glad I can make a contribution to the family finances for once. There's not much money in writing'.

Then there's the storm about to hit our fragile world. Parallel importation, which Mr Turnbull has indicated a liking for. The Productivity Commission has delivered an Interim Report recommending Australia adopts the practice—that it scrap parallel-import rules on books. The situation now is that publishers with local rights must supply books within a fortnight of publication overseas, or else shops may import them from any other market. Proponents argue that the removal of restrictions will cut prices.

It will not.

One of the only countries in the world foolish enough to adopt the practice of parallel importation is New Zealand. The result? Book prices did not fall. They are now more expensive, relatively, than Australia. Profits are now channelled into offshore companies, depriving local publishers of vital income. Those publishers have been forced to cut staff and book lists.

A few years back HarperCollins was publishing fifty books a year in New Zealand, now the figure is fifteen. Think about it. All those vividly local voices silenced. The tragically short-sighted parallel importation move has resulted in a collapse in New Zealand's publishing industry. Does Australia really want to follow suit? And of course, a nation like Britain wouldn't dream of introducing the measure—the British value their local literary industry too much, and want to preserve their dynamically varied, national voice at all costs.

The price of books in Australia has already substantially fallen over the past decade. I ask the Productivity Commission, how cheap is too cheap, if it costs us our future stories? Stories that create jobs; that contribute to the national conversation; that challenge and arrest us, inspire and move us; lift our spirits by having our own reality reflected back to us in a language we understand.

Who exactly is on this shadowy Commission, whose very title conjures up a Kafkaesque world of destruction masquerading as progress? I guarantee it would be no 'creator', for the body has not demonstrated any understanding of how the local book industry works. How writers are compensated. How a flourishing literary culture is nourished.

If parallel importation were allowed, there could conceivably be several editions of my *Bride Stripped Bare* or *Cleave* in the marketplace. An Australian edition—published by a local publisher with profits channelled back to that publisher—would be competing with an American and/or British edition, possibly even an Indian one, with all profits going back to the host country. And I, as the writer, wouldn't be getting as big a royalty—it would be a lower 'export' royalty, as opposed to a healthier home market one. The local music industry was decimated by this practice. Will our book industry follow suit?

And when I've been published overseas, distinct Australian words have been transformed into Brit or Yank speak to make it easier for the foreign reader. So 'stroller' became 'push chair', 'ute' became 'pickup truck'. Ghastly. Clunky and suspicious to the Aussie eye. This is what local readers can expect to see in Australian stories if parallel importation is introduced here. Our consumers, who are passionate about their local industry, need to be able to read their own stories in their own beautifully distinct and extremely colourful language.

The Productivity Commission also recommends the US system of 'fair use' of copyright material. The Commission's wording is vague, and it feels like it has the imprimatur of tech giants like Apple and Google breathing down its neck with this one. But the Commission is suggesting allowing use of some writing without payment to copyright holders—i.e. the authors. The Commission makes a suggestion, and of course it is only a suggestion, that Australian novels have their copyright lifted after, say, fifteen or twenty-five years. It has declared its colours with this one—this is what it thinks is best, despite it being impossible to implement under current international trading laws.

And it would be my retirement income demolished. I haven't earned superannuation since becoming a full-time writer; most of us don't. My world is purely freelance. No security. No workplace benefits. The writer's lot. I still

most gratefully receive royalties from my early novels *Shiver,
Cleave* and *The Bride Stripped Bare*, but if the Productivity
Commission had its way, I wouldn't for much longer. As
Charlotte Wood recently tweeted: 'Ok I'm off again to write
my new novel, which I may own for max 25 years if the
productivity commission has its way. Bye. #futility.'

A mate who's been an Australian literary agent for
decades recently emailed:

> The issues of fair dealing, parallel imports and period of
> copyright rear their heads on a regular basis, but in over
> 30 years I have never seen such a flawed report. By any
> comparison, books are now cheap in this country com-
> pared to anywhere else. As it is, the drop in prices has
> had a dramatically adverse impact on writers' income.
> I have seen my clients' income reduced by factors that
> would create a huge outcry if it happened in any other
> industry. The adoption of any of the Commission's
> recommendations would be the final nail in the coffin,
> and the new Dark Age will descend upon us even more
> quickly than it appears to be doing. The clincher in the
> Report, for me, was the claim that 'the consumer drives
> creativity'. Absurd and flawed thinking at its greatest.
> Look at TV ratings, and if we left it to consumers there
> would be wall-to-wall reality and cooking shows. I must
> say that it is all getting to me as I see my writer clients
> struggle more and more, and I myself try to hang in by
> the skin of my nails. All too depressing.

Australian writers want to ring-fence our literary
heritage—enable our creators and publishers to blossom

within a vibrantly local industry. Malcolm Turnbull wants ideas and innovation, but he risks unravelling the very model that rewards this creativity. As for our students in schools around the nation, topping their English classes and dreaming of one day becoming part of the national conversation, of writing the Great Australian Novel, well, they're unlikely to make a living out of that world. It's the grim reality for most of our nation's writers. $12 900. And if the Productivity Commission has its way that figure will be dropping a lot further as vital local publishers shut up shop, and advances and lists shrink even further. The Australian Government would have demonstrated a foolishness that the United States and the United Kingdom wouldn't dream of. To them, writers matter. To the Productivity Commission, they do not. Voices. Silenced.

Morris Gleitzman

Dear Australian Government,

I'm writing this letter because soon the Productivity Commission will recommend that you hurt Australian books, although they won't put it that way.

They will also recommend that you hurt Australian children. I'm pretty sure the Productivity Commissioners don't actually want books or children to be hurt, but they have to deal with a huge amount of information in their jobs and sometimes they miss things.

I'm hoping they'll notice the outcomes about books and children before they send you their report, but in case they don't, I thought I should mention it to you as I'm sure you don't want to hurt books or children either.

Before I go into more detail, I should probably tell you a bit about myself. I've been an Australian children's author for about thirty years and have published thirty-seven books.

I write fiction primarily for eight- to twelve-year-olds, though many of my books are also read by teenagers. All my books are published first in Australia and most are also published overseas with about twenty countries having their own editions of one or more of my titles.

Over the years, I've spoken about reading and writing and books in approximately fifteen-hundred schools. In many of them I've listened to young Australians talk about the importance of stories in their lives.

What they've said has left me convinced that stories are the single most important part of a young person's education, apart from teachers. In fact I'll go further and say that without stories, young people won't develop nearly as much confidence, entrepreneurial spirit, creativity, resilience, empathy, problem-solving ability, imaginative muscle-power and skill with words as they will with a rich and varied diet of stories. Or as much, I hope you're listening Productivity Commissioners, productivity.

I know what you're thinking, Australian Government. Of course he'd say that, he writes the things. Where's the evidence?

I do have evidence, though not as compelling as the evidence you could hear from several hundred thousand young Australians. But I'll do my best. Before I get onto my evidence, though, I must backtrack for a moment.

You've been contacted recently by most of the book publishers in Australia, who've let you know in detail how the changes to the publishing laws you've decided to make, cleverly even before the Productivity Commission advises you to make them, aren't very good changes. As a result of them we might pay a bit less, maybe, for some overseas books. But also as a result quite a few Australians will lose their jobs and we'll be left with a gravely injured publishing industry, possibly a dying one.

I don't have much to add to what the publishers have told you, other than a bit of preventative first-aid advice based on personal experience which I'll share with you later in this letter.

First, some evidence of what young Australians will lose as a result of these changes. Over several thousand years stories have developed and adapted, a bit like governments only faster, to meet the needs of the people they serve. This is especially true of stories for young people.

Stories for young people are some of the most gloriously varied and imaginative filaments in the literary light bulbs that illuminate our lives. But amidst their innovation and luminescence, most have certain traditional elements, tropes and plot points.

Usually a young character is confronted by a problem bigger and more threatening than any they've faced before. To solve or survive the problem, they must develop skills and qualities beyond their previous experience or homework. They must think bravely and honestly about themselves and the problem. They must hone their research skills to better understand what they're up against. Big problems require teamwork, so the character needs to form friendships and alliances. Understanding enemies is a help too. All of which requires development of interpersonal skills, in particular empathy. Creative thinking is a must because the young character needs to develop problem-solving strategies, and resilience is essential because big problems never get solved first time round, particularly when an author is contracted to write 250 pages. Which gives the young character plenty of opportunities to experience just how useful mistakes are.

When I talk with teachers about this classic character journey, their eyes light up. Very quickly they spot how many of these key elements are also crucial stages in a young person's education and personal development. The eyes of the business community light up too, because they can see how powerfully these stories model creative risk-taking, the innovative and profitable use of personal capital and the safeguarding of all shareholders, including pets.

Free-market enthusiasts see this also, but they tend to be more sceptical. 'All very well, Morris', they say, 'but these qualities aren't only found in Australian stories for young people, they're also found in the imported overseas stories that we calculate will be up to 9.5 per cent cheaper once territorial copyright is abolished'.

The teachers, all on tight budgets, are interested to hear this, and the business community too, particularly those with warehouses big enough to hold eight hundred thousand copies of a superseded Disney tie-in colouring book.

Which is when I remind them how crucial and irreplaceable Australian stories are to Australian young people. Just as American stories are to American young people, Slovenian stories to Slovenian young people, and so on.

Young Australians need far more from stories than just the chance to save a few dollars and cents. They need what only stories reflecting the truths and possibilities of their own lives can offer—help and inspiration to achieve maximum selfhood, maximum independence and, because this is important too, right Australian Government, maximum future economic productivity.

Every young person has to begin, at some stage in their primary school years, the most important and challenging journey of their life. The journey from somebody else's world to their own world. From the world that belongs to the adults who have nurtured them, to the world, internal and external, of their own dreaming and their own making.

It's an exciting journey but it can be tough and confusing. Stories about other young people making the same journey can help a lot. But if all that our kids get to read are stories from elsewhere, if they don't see anything of their own worlds championed and validated, if the message they get from their reading is that nothing from their world is worth putting in a story, how confusing and demoralising and unhelpful and counterproductive is that?

Which, Australian Government, is why I'm writing this letter. Territorial copyright isn't an evil plot to destroy the free market and the free world. It's a bit of chook wire over the seedbed of our literature and our culture. To allow our stories to take root, flourish and grow into big, strong, world's-best-practice stories.

My books have sold several million copies in Australia and several million more around the world. I'm an exporter. I'm glad my work makes a positive contribution to our balance of trade. And territorial copyright helped make that possible.

I wouldn't have got started without an Australian publisher. Nearly thirty years ago I started publishing with Pan Macmillan, and they lost a lot of money on me over the first couple of years. I still marvel at the resources they had to find to get me started. Editing, publicity, marketing, travel, stationery (I used to steal heaps), and everything else needed to make my books as good as possible and to persuade people to read them.

They took a big risk on me. It was helpful to them that when they finally found overseas markets for my books in the English-speaking world, they didn't have to face the prospect of artificially cheap copies of those US or UK editions coming back into Australia and undercutting the sales of their own editions of my books and sending them broke.

If you think I'm exaggerating, here's an example from later in my career. A few years ago, a couple of my books were picked up by one of the big US school book clubs. Approximately three hundred thousand extra copies of the US edition of those books were printed, and the book club bought them for a few cents above print cost because with those kinds of numbers a few cents is deemed to be a reasonable profit margin. But what if the book club misjudged demand and found they had even 10 per cent of the print run left at the end of their sales exercise? They'd be happy to sell them to a remainders wholesaler at print cost, probably no more than a dollar a copy. And where would the wholesaler look to dump those copies? The place where there's maximum demand for my books of course. Australia.

Yes, Productivity Commission, they might sell here a bit more cheaply than my Australian editions. But the sale of each one would prevent the sale of an Australian copy, and prevent my Australian publisher from recouping some of the cash they've spent bringing Australian stories to Australian young people. My stories and the stories of many other Australian authors. Stories that will help equip our young people, if I might indulge in a moment of pride, to build a healthy and vibrant nation in the future.

Please don't make the mistake of thinking that just because I'm one of the fortunate authors with thirty years' experience and healthy sales around the world, I don't need as many resources from a publisher. I publish with Penguin Random House these days, have done for twenty years, and their professional team is as crucial to my work as is a theatre team to a surgeon or an engineering team to a pilot or a policy and ethics team to a government minister. Together we strive for the excellence that young Australians deserve and insist on. I'm writing my thirty-eighth book, and I need good editing as much as I did with the first.

I'm proud to be one of the authors these days whose book sales help an Australian publisher support new Australian authors. Getting them started today is even harder and more resource-demanding than when I kicked off. Luckily we get a helping hand from overseas authors, and they don't mind at all, I've checked. Territorial copyright allows Australian publishers to sell their own editions of some overseas books, and the profits help our publishers get our new authors up and running.

During those early years when my middle names were Negative Fiscal Outcome, one of Pan Macmillan's big-selling overseas authors was Wilbur Smith. The sales of their local editions of his books helped get me started. I've never met Wilbur, but if I ever do I'll thank him heartily for the plane ticket to the Perth Writers Festival and the stationery.

Please also don't think that just because territorial copyright affords a bit of protection, Australian publishers aren't efficient and competitive. They are very efficient and very competitive. In this country we have a small fraction of the world's English-speaking population, and yet every year

Australian books make an impact throughout the English-speaking world and beyond. Books only reach that level of excellence and visibility when authors are supported by efficient and competitive publishers.

If you're still not convinced, Australian Government, take a peek at the sums you spend winning the hearts and minds of overseas folk when they're thinking about where to go for their holidays. Australian authors and publishers reach hearts and minds too. At this moment, all over the world, people are sitting with an Australian book, their hearts and minds full of what they're reading. Some of them have hearts so full they are weeping, some are chuckling, some are telling friends how their lives have been changed by the Australian book they've just finished and some are thinking that any country that can produce a book that good might just be worth a visit.

Australian publishers do not have Tourism Australia's international marketing budget. And yet they get their books to Frankfurt and Bologna and the other international book fairs, get them into the hands of regional publishers who complete the Australian hearts and minds supply chain. Efficient, I hope you'll agree, and inspiringly competitive.

If you abolish territorial copyright, Australian Government, you'll be kicking Australian publishers in the teeth. And much as you might like to do that, because much of the most articulate and widely read criticism of your industry comes from ours, please pause and consider the other outcomes.

Here's a short-term economic one. If you mortally wound my Australian publisher, I and lucky authors like me can move to or regularly visit England or the United States and publish from there. I have a readership for my Australian stories in the United Kingdom that would allow me to continue to write them for a UK publisher. But I would no longer be an Australian exporter. And all my Australian sales would become imports. My new middle names would be Net Drain On Our Balance Of Trade.

Most Australian authors, present and future, don't have that opportunity. They'd be left to flounder in the vast unmediated unedited unprofessional online self-publishing world in which there are undoubted pearls, but trying to find them and trying to be found makes the Pacific Ocean look like a duckpond.

To finish, Australian Government, just a couple more points.

The recommendations you're going to receive from the Productivity Commission will be presented in a theoretical framework in which an oft-cited concept is something called externalities. Externalities, I gather, are anything irrelevant to the prevailing economic theory. Some examples of externalities, if I've got this right, are art, kindness, imagination and love. Any human society that thinks it can organise its transactions successfully while excluding these is being very foolish. We have a vast literature of stories in our culture, stories stretching back thousands of years, that illustrate why. Please try to find the time to read some of them alongside the Productivity Commission Report.

I've written to you today about the importance of stories in the development of young people. I've pointed to ways that Australian stories help equip young Australians for productive lives. Truly productive lives. It is possible to have a childhood in which there are no nourishing stories.

When that happens, it is never the child's fault. There may be people in your party room who had such a childhood. I beg you, as you take steps to increase the productivity of our nation and achieve fair outcomes for consumers, please don't do it in a way that condemns future generations of Australians to childhoods without Australian stories. That would be a tragedy beyond words. And it wouldn't, it really wouldn't, be productive.

Yours sincerely,

Morris Gleitzman

Kate Grenville
Finding Australian Stories

The proposed changes to copyright have the potential to send Australian writing, in one lifetime, through an entire cycle from bust to boom and back to bust again. Sixty years ago, what Australians got to read was by and large dictated by people on the other side of the world. We were a literary colony. If the Productivity Commission has its way, we'll be back to that same second-hand status.

In my childhood nearly all the books I encountered came from Britain. They were by British writers, published and printed in Britain. They were about British people, British landscapes, British history.

My mother was a fierce nationalist with no great love for the Brits. She bought me all the British children's books—Enid Blyton, *Swallows and Amazons*, Rosemary Sutcliff and the rest. But she bought them with a certain reluctance—she knew that an Australian child's imagination and thinking ought to be excited not by the landscapes and people and histories of a place on the other side of the world, but by the place she was growing up in. So my mother scoured the bookshops for the few books that were about Australia. There was a handful of picture books—*Blinky Bill*, *Snugglepot and Cuddlepie*, *The Magic Pudding*. There was some of what you might call Australiana—the Billabong books, Henry Lawson. Good enough as far as it went, but that wasn't very far. Books about Australia were thin on the ground, compared to the rich variety of British books.

One reason was that Australia was a small place. Relative to Britain there weren't enough readers, there weren't enough writers. The small population made things difficult for an Australian publisher. (Back then there was essentially only one, Angus & Robertson, affectionately known to everyone as Gus & Bob's.) But what turned the difficult into the nearly impossible was the fact that, thanks to various cosy agreements between overseas publishers, the British controlled the Australian book market. Australian publishers were actively prevented from getting a foothold in international publishing. They couldn't publish books from overseas and they couldn't sell their own books to Britain. (As a British publisher told one of them as a self-evident truth, Australia was a place to sell books, but not a place to source them.)

This was sad news for an Australian publisher, but the real problem was what it meant for Australian authors. Even the most unworldly author could see what all that meant for his or her work. If authors wanted any chance of finding a readership both in and beyond Australia, they had to bypass the Australian publisher and go straight to where the only opportunity was: London.

Over there, the British publishers could cherrypick the few Australian books they wanted. Great books were among them, certainly—by Patrick White, Randolph Stow and Christina Stead, among others—but what the British thought mattered wasn't necessarily what mattered to Australian readers. The cherrypicking was done by foreigners—people with no knowledge of Australia and in most cases not much interest in it except as a place where people bought a lot of books. The books were edited on the other side of the world, too. Someone whose idea of Australia was no more than a set of stereotypes would be the one to decide which parts of the book were unimportant and should be cut, and which parts were significant and should be developed. They were likely to want to replace 'goanna' with 'iguana' and query what a dunny or a choko was. When that Australian author's books were exported to Australia, he or she was paid an 'export royalty': about a third of the normal royalty.

The book scene in Australia was one of the last leftovers of colonialism, and the consequences were what my mother found in the bookshops: our writing and publishing—and therefore our reading about ourselves—were undeveloped and stunted.

Then, during the 1960s and 1970s, things began to change—part of a global revolt against all kinds of colonialism. An author could now sell separate territorial licences to a book, and have different editions in the United Kingdom, the United States and Australia. Australian publishers were beginning to be able to buy and sell around the world. New Australian publishers began to appear, and some international publishers set up branches here that didn't just sell books but also published them.

Books about us began to appear in greater numbers and in more variety than ever before—books of analysis about

Australia like *The Lucky Country* or Robert Hughes' *The Art of Australia*; landmark plays about Australia such as *Summer of the Seventeenth Doll*; homegrown satire like *They're a Weird Mob*; and an unprecedented volume and variety of fiction titles.

These were books that no British publisher might have found worth publishing, but for the newly emerging Australian sense of identity they were formative. These were the books that gave us a way of talking about ourselves, of understanding ourselves, of having a conversation about ourselves as Australians—not as pretend-Britons—that we hadn't had before.

Some of the new Australian publishers were branches of international publishing houses, such as Penguin Australia, and some were new independent Australian publishers such as McPhee Gribble, the University of Queensland Press and Ure Smith. A mature literary industry began to take shape, run by people passionate about bringing Australian books to an Australian readership.

But the big international publishers were still running the show, because they still held the best cards for making money out of books in Australia. With their resources and their economies of scale, they could still shape the market. They continued to control the price and availability of books in Australia. Having our market controlled from the other side of the world made it very difficult for the small, under-resourced Australian publishers to risk long-term investment in authors.

For the author, it was a bind: if your book was of interest to the British, and you got a British publisher, you'd be earning those pitiful export royalties on every copy sold in Australia. On the other hand, if the book didn't find a British publisher, you'd be earning the full royalty, but your Australian publisher would be small and the prospects for your book would likely be limited.

That was why, in 1991, our ingenious 'use it or lose it' territorial copyright laws were passed. If a book is not made available in Australia very soon after its release elsewhere, then booksellers are free to bring in as many copies as they want. That means, if there's an Australian edition of a book, and it's published first, the Australian edition is the one that booksellers are obliged to sell in Australia.

It's a finely calibrated piece of legislation. It supports Australian publishers because they can invest in authors and books, confident that their edition won't be undercut by dumped imports or overseas remainder copies. It supports Australian authors, because they earn full royalties and have a committed, strong publisher who can afford to take a risk or two. It protects consumers, because it allows them to order individual copies from anywhere in the world, either through a bookshop or independently (the laws only apply to bulk orders). It also brings Australian publishing into line with that of other countries, where the local publisher has exclusive rights to the local market.

That law ushered in a gigantic period of growth for Australian writing and publishing because overnight, for the first time, Australian publishing made good business sense. It was no longer a cottage industry, but part of a global one.

Now we take it for granted that there's a wide range of independent Australian publishers who can afford to take a punt on unknown authors. We accept it as natural that the big international publishers have Australian offshoots, publishing Australian books rather than just selling us British or American ones. We don't realise what a new thing it is to have bookshops full of books by Australians, about Australia, working in our Australian frames of reference and in our own Australian kind of English. Our literary festivals are packed with people who come to hear fellow Australians talk about the world we share. Literary prizes invite readers to try out this year's crop of Australian headliners. A richly varied and robust literary world is something we now take as our birthright. And so we should.

Only if you grew up in the culturally colonised and impoverished Australia that oldies like me did, do you know just how fragile that wealth of culture really is. At one stroke of the legislative pen, our literary culture will start a slide back. Australian publishers will be the first to fade, unable to hold out against the flood of overseas editions of their own titles. But without strong Australian publishers, authors will suffer, too: publishers in London and New York might be happy to cherrypick, using their own views of what's important, but they have no particular interest—philosophical or financial—in Australian writing. They won't support the depth of book culture a grown-up nation needs. If we want to read Australian books, we need robust Australian publishers.

If the proposed changes are enshrined in law, before too long we'll be back to where we were sixty years ago, when a determined mother had to scour the bookshops to find a few Australian stories to feed the imagination of her Australian child.

Andy Griffiths

Food, Fighting and Funny Pictures: Growing Up with Australian Books

As a child I was fortunate enough to have a bookshelf filled with great books from all around the world, but Australian children's classics such as *The Magic Pudding* and *Cole's Funny Picture Books* spoke to me in a way that even at a young age I recognised as unmistakably Australian. It is difficult to define exactly what that 'Australian-ness' is. It's not just—or even—about seeing Australian animals or iconical Australian places and landmarks … it's broader and deeper than that. It's more of a feeling—a sort of free-wheeling knockabout charm that, like Vegemite, is instantly identifiable.

Knowing that some of the books I was reading were Australian made the whole business of book writing and my then barely articulated dream of perhaps one day writing my own books seem just that little bit more attainable.

My childhood writing consisted mostly of attempts to imitate the books I admired, and none were more influential than the *Cole's Funny Picture Books* produced by Melbourne writer 'Professor' EW Cole, who made compilations of funny stories and pictures in the hope that linking laughter and delight to a child's earliest reading experiences would encourage them to associate reading with pleasure, thus increasing the likelihood that they would grow up to be lifelong readers.

It certainly worked for me. By the time I was twelve I had taught myself to touch-type on a 1920s Underwood typewriter and was producing a regular edition of a 3-page magazine consisting of jokes, riddles, funny stories and pictures. I sold my publication to my classmates for three cents a copy (a price that covered the cost of production—paper and ink and spirits for the fordigraph machine).

This early experience in self-publishing was to stand me in good stead for kickstarting my own career as a writer many years later when, as a high school English teacher, I identified a need for books with the sort of boisterously absurd, take-no-prisoners humour that had been so inspiring for me as a child. I began to write simple short stories which I compiled into photocopied booklets for my students to read and imitate. The stories I was writing then—as now—are a melting pot of elements from my own favourite childhood books and comics, infused with what I consider quintessentially Australian attitudes, such as a penchant for irony and understatement, an ingrained suspicion of authority and a delight in rebelling against good taste.

I'll be the first to admit that these early self-published booklets were rough and very much the work of a beginning writer wrestling with the complex demands of both fiction writing and humour, but they excited my students and began to turn their attitude to writing and reading from negative to positive.

These booklets and their positive reception also began to make that barely conscious dream of being a writer a little more conscious and I began devoting many hours a day to writing practice as well as to reading books about writing and taking short courses at the then newly established Victorian Writers' Centre. The more I wrote and studied, however, the more I became aware that the left-of-centre humour that appealed to me and my students was quite different to the officially sanctioned serious literature that was winning awards and attracting grants.

Not that this was a problem. I've never believed that the world owes me a living, and with a mentor like EW Cole and a number of positive experiences in self-publishing (made even easier by the appearance of the first word processors and the ubiquity of photocopiers) I decided that that was the path to follow. In 1991 I produced a compilation of all my stories to that point—illustrated by a friend—and sold 500 copies at $10 each. As with the magazine I had sold to my classmates, the price of this book covered the cost of production and no more. It did, however, gain me a wider audience than my classroom and, importantly, my first reviews, which helped me to work out what I was doing right and how to do it better.

The advantage of self-publishing is the freedom to publish exactly what you like. The disadvantage is distribution: how to physically get the books into bookshops, pick up the cash and process returns. (Many a self-publisher with a garage or spare room full of their works will attest to this difficulty.) Gradually, however, partly as a result of my self-publishing efforts, I attracted the interest of commercial publishers—firstly educational publisher Longman Cheshire, who published my work as a creative writing textbook, then Reed for Kids, who published my first book of fiction and, soon after, Pan Macmillan Australia, who have been my publisher for eighteen years now.

The process I have just described of moving from self-publishing to having books published by Pan Macmillan took ten years and was funded by my own savings. As I said, I never thought the world owed me a living and I was realistically modest about my ability to attract a large audience with my left-of-centre humour so, to help pay the bills, I developed my skills as a visiting author and writing workshop teacher in schools.

I am very happy to acknowledge, however, the enormous support I have received from my Australian publisher, Pan Macmillan, from the beginning of my career up to the present day.

Pan Macmillan's belief in the value of touring authors as a slow but sure means of developing an audience has been the making of me as a writer. As well as funding large marketing campaigns, they have organised a national tour for every book I have published with them since 1998—often two (and sometimes three!) tours in a single year—as well as contributing to the cost of my attendance at countless writing festivals around the country.

A typical promotional book tour can last anywhere from two to five weeks and involves talks and signings at bookshops, libraries and schools in all capital cities and many major regional centres. Pan Macmillan undertakes the full funding of the planning, travel and hotel costs, as well as providing a full-time publicist for the entire length of the tour.

In the early years of my career, in the late 1990s and early 2000s, bookshop appearances would attract a small number of readers, and would only result in a relatively modest number of book sales. These early tours were undertaken by both Pan Macmillan and myself with the view to the longer term and would definitely have cost the company more than it received in book sales.

These tours, however, were invaluable in allowing me to establish personal relationships with booksellers across the country, and to hear firsthand about their experiences selling books in general, and my books in particular. As a result of these interactions with both booksellers and readers, I was able to continually hone my craft as a writer and presenter. I believe this 'conversation' between myself, the reader and booksellers/librarians/teachers and parents has been crucial to my development as a writer and would not have been possible without Pan Macmillan's long-term investment in my career.

The results of this long-term investment have been that, along with illustrator/co-writer Terry Denton and editor/ co-writer Jill Griffiths, I have been able to create books that communicate powerfully to a very large readership.

Last year, the fifth book in our Treehouse series, *The 65-Storey Treehouse*, was not only the fastest-selling Australian book in a decade but also the bestselling book in any category in Australia. At book signings around the country we were overwhelmed with readers, resulting in signing queues that lasted for three to five hours almost every day for four weeks. To date, the series has sold well over two million copies in Australia and over a million internationally.

This didn't happen overnight; it happened over eighteen years and, I hope, serves to illustrate the extraordinary results that can be gained from long-term investment in Australian authors.

Until the Treehouse series, my books had relatively limited success in other countries and were rarely translated. However, the Treehouse series has now been sold into twenty-four countries and is already a bestselling (and award-winning) series in Norway, Holland and Korea. Last month it debuted on *The New York Times* bestsellers list. This is obviously all very welcome news and confirmation of what I have long believed: that, given the right conditions and plenty of time to grow and develop, Australian authors are capable of producing books the equal of any in the world.

This could be a mixed blessing, however, if parallel importation restrictions (PIRs) are scrapped. These restrictions prohibit booksellers from importing a foreign edition of a book if an Australian publisher has purchased the rights to publish an Australian edition of the book and does so within thirty days of its publication overseas.

I'm not looking for an easy ride for either myself or my publisher, but I am most definitely looking for a level playing field. I want Australian publishers to be able to confidently invest in Australian authors without the possibility that if these authors are subsequently published overseas that these overseas editions—produced in larger quantities for larger populations and therefore at a lower cost per unit—would then be imported by Australian booksellers to compete with Australian editions.

This would reduce the returns to the Australian publishers who took the financial risk of helping to develop the books in the first place. The ultimate effect of this could be to make investment in new Australian authors less attractive and, at the very least, mean a vast reduction in the amount of money that publishing companies have available to take a chance on fostering new Australian talent or to create opportunities to bring authors and readers/booksellers/librarians together.

Publishing is a highly speculative enterprise. Often it is not clear which books will sell until they are actually published. As a result, many books do not even earn back the advance the publisher pays the author and it's the relatively few books that do very well that allow the publisher to absorb these losses and operate at a profit.

Leading bookseller Mark Rubbo says in the June 2016 edition of *Readings Monthly*, 'If bookshops are to survive they need to be places that people feel a connection to and want to spend time in. They need to be what the American sociologist Ray Oldenburg described as the "third place"; they must be "anchors" of community life that facilitate and foster broader, more creative interaction'.

And one of the most powerful ways for bookshops to facilitate this creative interaction is to have regular author events ... for which they rely on publishers with the resources and incentive to invest in publishing and promoting local authors.

Australia is a relatively small market, which means print runs are correspondingly smaller and unit costs per book higher. If we are to keep a level playing field and give Australian publishers and emerging writers a fair chance to compete with the best in the world, we need the PIRs to remain in force.

I also don't believe that book consumers are driven solely by price. As a book consumer myself I don't like to pay more for books than strictly necessary, but not at any cost, not if it means threatening Australian bookshops and the ongoing incentive for Australian publishers to make a long-term investment in publishing and growing Australian authors. (And it's not as if the consumer does not have a choice already—my and many other books are readily available at significantly reduced prices from discount department stores.)

It seems reckless to threaten a system that allows Australian authors to both connect with Australian readers and to compete on the world stage simply to provide cheaper books to Australian consumers—especially when such an outcome cannot be guaranteed. (The scrapping of PIRs in New Zealand has not reduced book prices significantly, but it has had a detrimental effect on the publishing and bookselling industry.)

As an author, a child can pay me no higher compliment than to tell me that my books have made them love reading or that I have inspired them to want to be a writer too. I would like Australian children (and adults) to continue to have Australian books that give them pleasure and inspire them to read and write and dream.

Jane Harper

Winning the Victorian Premier's Literary Award for an Unpublished Manuscript has been a wonderful experience for me from start to finish. But the award also created a much wider circle of very real benefits and opportunities. I think too often we make the mistake of viewing creative awards as something that benefits the winner alone, and risk overlooking the bigger picture.

Since winning, it has become very obvious how much one opportunity breeds another. Publishing a book not only generates editing and printing work and hopefully sales for local booksellers, but creates a positive ripple effect of other job opportunities. For example, the designer commissioned to design the cover for the Australian edition of *The Dry* was able to sell the design to the US publishers, and actors and sound technicians have been paid to record the audio version of the novel.

The Dry has also been sold overseas and through that has been transformed from a creative work into an export product. When I get money from overseas publishers, I get paid in Australian dollars and I pay taxes on that income here in Australia.

At a time when the Productivity Commission is recommending changes that will have a serious and long-lasting impact on the health of the Australian publishing industry, and at a time when we are being urged as a nation to move away from our reliance on the resources sector and embrace the 'ideas boom', what better example of this is there than the spark of an idea that in turn becomes a manuscript, that becomes a book and a product that can be sold in Australia and exported overseas?

The $15 000 seed money that I won as a prize last year has turned into something many times over that thanks to the Australian publishing industry, and on any metric— creative, economic and jobs-wise—it has been a success. I urge governments of either persuasion to recognise that and continue to support writers and the Australian publishing industry for years to come.

Chloe Hooper
Suggested Edits: 2017

Dear Ms Hopper,

Thank you for submitting this fascinating article. It's a great start, but we wonder if you've considered moving the location to better suit an international audience? This could work wonderfully well in a 'hardscrabble' Anglo-Irish context, or you might like to pursue our suggestions below!

In a bunker-like hall in ~~Townsville, North Queensland~~, [**Let's reassess!**] a boxing ring is set up under fluorescent strip lights and the crowd sit in monsoonal heat, watching two ten-year-old ~~Aboriginal~~ boys punching the stuffing out of each other. One minute they look like gladiators in oversized gloves and helmets, belting hard at the other's head; then, when they fall half-crying with exhaustion into each other's arms, like brothers caught fighting in their bedroom.

By one corner of the ring stands Ray Dennis, seventy-one, ~~the coach of the all Aboriginal Palm Island Boxing Team.~~ Dennis has the look of a man just hit. His nose, four times broken, has found a new position on his face; rust-rimmed glasses hang there at an angle. At ten he went to primary school for the first time and got badly bullied. At fifteen he bought boxing gloves and started training. Each session left him with a busted-up mouth, but he kept going until he could beat grown men; until, in 1956 he was runner-up to represent ~~Australia~~ at the Olympics. Later he worked as a **janitor**, **short order cook, debt collector** ~~drycleaner, at a meatworks, in construction~~—and all the time he trained other boxers. 'I never done anything spectacular', he'll say. Nothing that is but train three generations to win a hundred or so state and national boxing titles.

Ten years ago, Ray Dennis found himself out of work. **[Have edited slightly, hope this works for you!]** Each day he made more ~~homebrew~~ **moonshine in an old abandoned barn up on Copperhead Road, usin' corn and whatever else he came by, and started killing himself drinking it. Then he remembered the talent of the young men he'd trained** from ~~Palm Island—the Aboriginal ex-mission community east of Townsville.~~ **all over the Smoky Mountains. Sitting on his** ~~verandah~~ **porch, watching the blue mist hovering around the peaks and valleys, he vowed right then he would train an Olympic medalist. In the beginning he put a boxing ring in an abandoned cotton field and started teaching the sons and nephews of his old protégés. More kids came and sometimes after training they'd take out** their banjos, and Uncle Ray still knew how to make the harmonica sing, and the sound of that sweet old bluegrass would melt their cares clean away.

Surrounded by the oak forests of the southern Appalachians, those mighty northern reds and scarlets, and the hickories, he could feel himself start to breathe again. One day a girl came out of the huckleberry shrub and stood watching the boys in the ring. Noby Clay was seventeen, a radiant, delicate-limbed girl who'd followed her brother to boxing training and asked Ray Dennis if she could have a turn. She was a natural, picking up everything Ray taught her immediately, 'firing off perfect punches'. She came back every day and Ray encouraged her to give up smoking marijuana and street fighting. Then, with her life straightened out, Noby started having babies.

[Any other backstory? For example, did trainer ever fall off wagon? Perhaps he cleans up and goes to see boxer in a Motel 6 room; she's, say, been working as a cleaner all along Highway 441. He convinces her she should fight again. If she trains she can do it! He finds a babysitter for her kids: a montage of unlikely but trustworthy childcare workers—endearing? Then add from original:] Dennis was one of the few people in her life Noby had been able to rely on. 'Every time I go [to training], he be there. No matter what time. It could be raining, could be hot, he'd be there. I go there, he be there.' She tells me she had told him after the fight, 'You never give up on me so I won't give up on you'.

Tonight will be her first fight in five years. [Olympics at stake, yes?]

Now twenty-five she sits next to her ~~pram~~ baby stroller, in which 11-week-old Lorna, her third child, lies on a fleece covered by a white blanket with pink and purple hearts. Noby has just fed Lorna, and even with the baby on her breast, she moves lightly from one foot to the other, staying loose, starting the dance. Ringside she tries to calm herself, listening to the rapper Soulja Boy on her phone: *Now you watch me! Now you watch me! Now you watch!*

Sitting two rows behind the ~~Palm Islanders~~ is the ~~Tasmanian~~ ALASKAN team, wearing matching green and gold uniforms. How to say this? If you were casting a group of white supremacists, you might consider recruiting from gyms in outer suburban ~~Hobart~~ JUNEAU. These men have shaved heads, or hair close-cropped with long rat's tails, and muscular, crossed arms bearing heavy-duty tattoos: a wolf's head donning an Indian chieftain's feathered head-dress, a samurai wrestling a tiger, an Aztec warrior, Chinese symbols, tributes to other boxers, stars, scorpions, skulls vomiting jewels—~~everything, basically, bar a dot-painting of an Aboriginal Dreamtime Spirit~~. And sitting among them is a creamy skinned, 17-year-old lightweight called Rebecca Miller about to have her first fight with Noby Clay.

Noby turns around and sticks out her hand to introduce herself: 'I'm Noby, like Moby Dick, but with an N'. She asks Rebecca how she's finding the weather?

Noby stands and pushes the ~~pram~~ stroller to the make-shift change rooms to get ready. Around her, sleek teenage boys, their skin shimmering with sweat, skip furiously, or punch at the fetid air. Noby finds a corner for Lorna's ~~pram~~ stroller and stretches on the concrete floor, limbering up. Her hair in a bun at the nape of her neck, she's more ballerina than boxer.

Ray Dennis comes to help Noby prepare. He starts wrapping Noby's hands with old black bandages and he looks like he's going to cry. He looks like a father about to give away his daughter: proud, nervous, slightly forlorn. He loves her and she loves him. Noby's own father saw her when she was six months old and they have not met again. Ray finishes, and she raises a strapped fist to his face, softly wiping the sweat from his brow. [**Yes! More of this ✔**]

Opposite, in another jerry-rigged cubicle, three men prepare Rebecca Miller for the fight. Rebecca has been training hard for six months; working out in three **sweaters** ~~jumpers~~; sparring in a sauna to ready herself for the heat. Still, when she stepped off the plane into the ~~Townsville~~ humidity she found she couldn't breathe. She's never left ~~Tasmania~~ **ALASKA** before. ~~All she knows about Aboriginal culture is from a DVD a high school teacher once showed the class about 'how they lived way back and that. It was different'.~~ Now she sits while the men massage her legs then help her dress. They secure the breast protector. She has diamante earrings and a diamante in her belly button. She removes them and the men tie the lacy cummerbund of her boxing shorts, they knot her high red boxing boots. Then Rebecca stands and starts to spar: one, two; one, two; one, two. The air doesn't move at all. She's red-faced, determined: one, two. Other **ALASKANS** ~~Tasmanians~~ come and act as bodyguards, folding their arms, making a tattooed barricade so she can't be seen by her opponent.

~~Meanwhile Noby and the boys from Palm Island are goofing around, laughing.~~

~~The ring has red, white and blue ropes; Australian flags fly in each corner.~~ The coaches strap on the women's gloves, giving them their mouthguards, their headgear. Both look grave.

The bell rings. 'Round one!'

Rebecca comes straight for Noby. She keeps her fists close to her face, her shoulders high. She bounces on her feet and her hair in a high **braid** ~~plait~~ sticks out of her helmet, bobbing up and down. She's engine driven, fierce: she aims for Noby's face. But the thing is, being hit relaxes Noby. Noby's arm seems to grow longer and she punches hard. 'Once I taste her hit and she taste mine, I'm right. I'm right then.'

Rebecca is stronger, 12 kilograms heavier and fitter. She gets Noby on the ropes and keeps hitting rhythmically— one, two; one, two—as if in a boxercise class.

The crowd cheers—there's no sense that two women fighting is out of the ordinary, ~~but as Noby explains, 'the life-style on Palm is plain and simple: you live to fight, you fight to live'.~~ Still, by the end of the second round, Ray Dennis, in the corner, is ready to throw in the towel. It pains him to see Noby taking hits, but after each bout she comes back to the corner and insists on continuing: 'People like her don't want to give in'.

In the third round Noby isn't moving—she's scared her legs will give way—but now she can read Rebecca's style. Noby's on the ropes, but she's not done for. She knows what Rebecca's going to do: one, two; one, two. She lets her land the first hit but as soon as Rebecca goes to land her second one, Noby weaves under and punches Rebecca in the ribs. Then again. Then a third time.

Before long the women look like wind-up toys. But Noby is losing energy, her movements become slower, jerkier; she's running out of power, while Rebecca just keeps pounding.

At last the bell sounds. The referee separates the women. Noby immediately moves in to hug Rebecca who, surprised, instinctively jabs her in the ribs, under those breasts swollen with milk. Then she **recognizes** ~~recognises~~ the embrace and returns it, smiling, baring her big, white mouthguard. When Rebecca is declared the winner, the referee holds her hand in the air. Then Noby congratulates her and her coach, before climbing down from the ring and returns to the ~~pram~~ stroller, her lower lip bleeding and the flesh beneath one eye bruised. Later, she admits she knew she wasn't going to win: 'I just wanted to let people know I'm back'.

With Lorna in her arms, she finds Rebecca, surrounded by the other **ALASKANS** ~~Tasmanians~~, and with utter warmth and charm shows them all her baby. Rebecca, still doused in sweat, a gold medal round her neck, coos and smiles at the infant, wholeheartedly admiring her.

[ENDING TO BE DISCUSSED!]

~~As the night progresses, the older Palm Island boys, then more senior boxers step into the ring. This is family entertainment in Townsville. Barefoot toddlers roam around, following bigger kids who play on the fight's margins, while their parents watch on, hungry for a knockout. The hall's alive with bloodlust and camaraderie. It's mad, all of it. Waiting for the rains, everyone is covered in sweat. It's like we're all together in a fever and as the delirium kicks in I see things I wasn't expecting.~~

~~The Palm Island boys stand talking to the white boys they've just been fighting. They're locked in conversation, joking, laughing.~~

~~None of the Palm kids know why their families were sent to the island—just as Rebecca Miller doesn't know how~~

her family ended up in Tasmania. Whatever Reconciliation means in other parts of the country, here it is taking place between people who may not even know why they need to reconcile; people who don't have much but are making the most of what they do; whacking each other without mercy while other black and white Australians dodge and weave in their seats, as if they too are in the ring. The boxers could be battling over the last two hundred years; then they take their gloves off and start talking.

Toni Jordan
The Colonial Edition

It's a strange kind of headline for us today, living in the era of Richard Flanagan and Liane Moriarty and Helen Garner and Michael Robotham. AUSTRALIAN NOVELISTS, the top line reads, and underneath: BOOKS PUBLISHED IN ENGLAND. It's not a front-page story, of course, literature is rarely that, but it's in a reasonable spot: page 18 in the Brisbane *Telegraph*, 10 July 1926. It says: 'The Australian novelist, Mr. Jack MacLaren, has published his twenty-fifth book, "The Isle of Escape", which is a sex story, set in the South Seas. His wife is publishing a novel dealing with reincarnation, entitled "Which Hath Been"'. (I'd love to read both of these—they seem perfect for me—but finding them isn't easy, as I'll explain.)

Success in London wasn't the only thing a novelist could achieve to get the press gushing. *The Argus*, 5 September 1941, excitedly noted AUSTRALIAN WOMAN NOVELIST'S

SUCCESS: Book Chosen By New York Club. 'The Book of the Month Club has unanimously selected the novel "The Timeless Land" by Eleanor Dark, of Katoomba (NSW), for distribution among members in October. It says that it is a brilliant work, which, it hopes, will make Australia's history more familiar to Americans.'

Once I began to look through newspapers and magazines from the last century, I found example after example like this: a 1935 obituary for Mrs Campbell Praed, who died in England aged eighty-six and was 'the first Australian-born novelist worthy of consideration in Australian literature'; *The Women's Weekly* of 12 May 1951, which told us that 'Young Australian Novelist Finds Success in London', about Catherine Gaskin; on 14 January 1947 *The Kalgoorlie Miner* told us that Christina Stead's success in the United States '... is another indication that Australia has come-of-age in the literary world'.

It seems that hardly any writers lived here in the twentieth century and, even if they did, it was their overseas publishing success that made the news. Up until the 1970s, Australian readers were sent 'colonial editions': editions of novels published in Britain, designed to disseminate British values and maximise British publishers' profits. Macmillan, the famous Scottish publishers, were particularly adept at this—they published Macmillan's Colonial Library series— but they weren't alone. Colonial editions meant that British publishers could make savings by ordering larger print runs and send the surplus overseas, and they had very few expenses in Australia. No pesky authors to edit or pay or market, for instance. The money, and the influence, stayed where it belonged.

Asserting a degree of cultural independence is difficult when you're a smallish English-speaking market with a commitment to a living minimum wage, dwarfed by the United States and the United Kingdom. We've long known this: when the Whitlam Government revamped the Australia Council for the Arts in the 1970s, it was 'to help establish and express an Australian identity through the arts and to promote an awareness of Australian culture abroad'. Gough also promised to 'review quotas for Australian television, cinema and book production and encourage a greater participation of Australian creative talent in their production'. Quotas, though, work better for some industries than others.

Commercial free-to-air television has a quota for Australian content. It's required by law to 'broadcast an annual minimum transmission quota of 55 per cent Australian programming between 6am and midnight on their primary channel … [and] provide during the same time at least 1460 hours of Australian programming on their non-primary channels', according to the Australian Communications and Media Authority website. The last time this policy was reviewed only two submissions were received, so it appears the quota is doing its job to achieve the authority's objective of 'developing and reflecting a sense of Australian identity, character and cultural diversity'.

The Australian film industry has developed along different lines: it receives direct government subsidies to help ensure we don't turn into the fifty-first state. Screen Australia, the body responsible, says it 'aims to inspire, inform and engage screen audiences through compelling Australian storytelling', so as well as tax incentives for investment, it funded seventy-one film projects in 2014–15, spending a total of more than $21 million. These films went on to sell in over one hundred territories; the government investment here proved not only important to developing world-class skills, but also enabled Australian culture to be exported around the world, which benefits our tourism, industrial and diplomatic efforts.

Books, though. As Aleksandr Solzhenitsyn said, 'Literature becomes the living memory of a nation'. So what can a responsible government do to ensure our thriving Australian publishing industry continues to reflect our culture to ourself and the world, and earns some export dollars while we're at it?

It's simple. Nothing.

No hundred-million-dollar-plus funding body for the publishing industry, no laws regulating the number of Australians they must publish. Nothing. Australians know what they want to read, thank you very much. If publishers here don't cater for them, they're more than capable of buying what they want online and having it shipped in, fast and cheap. The onus is on Australian writers, publishers and booksellers to satisfy Australian readers. If we don't, we'll all be out of business.

The novelist Jonathan Franzen, on hearing of the government's plans to unilaterally open the Australian book market, said, 'Even America is not so slavishly subservient to a theory of the free market that we don't protect our authors, our booksellers, and our publishers'. That our government would disrupt a $2.2 billion industry in favour of taxpayer handouts as an experiment in economic rationalism, when the United States and the United Kingdom won't do the same, is Kafkaesque. It would return us to the days of the Colonial Edition.

I love a good sex story, so I've been looking in second-hand stores and online for Jack MacLaren's 1926 novel *Isle of Escape*, ever since I first heard of it. I've never seen a single copy. *Which Hath Been: A Novel of Reincarnation* by Mrs Jack MacLaren (really) is available, but it sells out of New York for more than US$100, not including shipping. I'm an Australian, living in Australia, looking for two novels written by Australians. It seems I'm destined never to read them.

Thomas Keneally

Because I was on book tour in Britain as this volume was put together, I had to fall back on the following fairly staid piece I wrote for the *Australian Financial Review*. There were some images cut from the piece which would have been tolerated in a more robust piece. For example, I described the Australian publishing industry as existing on a narrow ledge of guaranteed time. I am proud of what it has produced on that ledge. I celebrate the diverse commentary, the wealth of creation, now likely to be obliterated by a federal government trumpeting innovation. As the first step on that much-waited-for post-colonial road, they seek to obliterate the very industry equipped to interpret innovation to the citizenry. Similarly, I was tempted to call on Malcolm Turnbull to confront what he knew and cherished in his late, great uncle, Robert Hughes, who would—I am sure—have counselled his nephew by marriage against such a fatal step. And there was one last image cut from the piece, perhaps an exorbitant one but one that's apposite. When I began to write, and I and other Australian writers, some older, some younger, were trying to create the craft of letters as a modern profession in Australia, it seemed that a well-published Australian was almost as rare and as much a cause for surprise as a goanna riding a bicycle. It isn't any more, nor should it be.

It will be a bitter thing if all we bicycling goannas are driven off the landscape for the sake of a doctrinaire application of fundamentalist, terrorist economics to our ecology. No-one will or can replace us. The withering of a profession will be permanent, and voices yet to emerge will be stilled. But all that's said in what I wrote, and so, for what it's worth, here it is.

Productivity Commission Recommendation Threatens Livelihood of Book Industry

Like other Australians, I was excited when Malcolm Turnbull announced encouragement for innovation in Australia. How strange would it be if, at the inception of innovation policy, the very medium through which ideas are disseminated in Australia, the publishing industry, were eviscerated.

Sadly this is what we are facing.

The Productivity Commission draft report on intellectual property recommended the government repeal parallel import restrictions for books—to take effect no later than the end of 2017. Publishing and bookselling in Australia are subject to parallel importation rules (or restrictions, depending how you look at them). I hope that's the most boring sentence I ever have to write. The truth is though that PIR is a major factor in the Australia we have, in its identity, its cohesion, its heritage.

PIR represents the little ledge of copyright security, the small acre, on which we have created a respected publishing industry, one of the largest in the world, and a treasure house of writing of all kinds. On that said ledge, many successful books of Australian or international derivation enable the publication of more marginal Australian books and more risky ones—that is the way a healthy publishing industry is run.

It is worth saying that PIR does not restrict individual readers from buying books from anywhere in the world, and book retailers can order single copies from anywhere in the world on behalf of a customer. A customer has freedom in Australia under the current model but the law protects the industry from large-scale dumping.

As the law is now, if an Australian publishing company owns the rights to publish any book in Australia, section 37 of the *Copyright Act* of 1968 prohibits other people, major booksellers, for example, from importing commercial quantities of that book from other markets. According to law, the Australians have the right to publish their edition within a month of publication elsewhere. But in fact Australian publishers have agreed to produce their edition of any book within fourteen days of publication elsewhere. In November 2015 Treasurer Scott Morrison said the government supported the parallel importation of books but would progress the recommendation of the Productivity Commission after its report on the matter.

So what would that mean?

Take territorial copyright away, and the ecology of the Australian book world and the range of Australian books published will wither. 'Without parallel import restrictions, Australian publishers would be exposed to all the risks and failures but be unable to benefit from the successes', says a comprehensive report from Systems Knowledge Concepts on Australian publishing.

New Zealand repealed its PIR legislation in 1998. Since that time the New Zealand publishing industry has contracted disastrously. Even since 2008, according to Nielsen BookScan, the range of books published there has shrunk by more than a further third, and sales are down 16 per cent.

The cost of New Zealand books has risen since 2008, while Australian prices in 2015, under PIR, had fallen and were 18.2 per cent cheaper than New Zealand's. The orthodox priests of fundamental market economics have not produced a New Zealand miracle but a wasteland where once there was an industry, and a betrayal, as well, of New Zealand's literary inheritance.

Our industry produces more than seven thousand new books annually and generates $2 billion in revenue. More than one thousand businesses in Australia are engaged in the publishing industry, and directly employ more than four thousand people. Many are, of course, small businesses. Australia has the fourteenth largest publishing industry in the world and the largest independent bookseller section in the entire English-language market.

My friend the author Richard Flanagan was so concerned about the coming immolation that he got together with Peter Carey and myself and drafted a letter. By now

Flanagan's reputation is such that he would survive without the local market, but it was the market that grew him, and he loyally wanted to see it continue in existence. Of the proposed abolition of PIR, he wrote, 'The consequences will be job losses, public revenue losses when profits are transferred overseas, and a brutal reduction in the range of Australian books publishers will be able to publish. Australia will become a dumping ground for American and English books, and we will risk becoming—as we once were—a colony of the minds of others ... We are not asking for money, or for a subsidy.

'But as writers we ask for the same rules and intellectual property rights that prevail for writers and book publishing in the USA, in Britain, and in Europe.' The Americans and British have never contemplated abandoning their territorial copyright for the sake of economic fundamentalism. Nor should we!

And it cannot be irrelevant that books are not toothbrushes, as admirable for their purposes as toothbrushes are. Books are our magical doors, our personal treasures, cherished possessions loanable only to closest friends. In the name of the totalitarian Moloch of a free market, some are willing to cut out of the picture not only the present emerging writers of Australia, but writers of the future, and with them the wonders that could be created by them, the beloved artefacts of the spirit of our community.

From an article published in the Australian Financial Review, *29 April 2016*

David Malouf

Book Culture, a Delicate Balance

The ecology of a culture may be as fragile, as precariously balanced, as the one we call Nature. We should be very sure of how that balance has been achieved and continues to work before we think of adjusting or 'improving' it.

Australia's book culture, as I have observed it as a reader, then as a writer, over more than sixty years, is an unusually healthy one. It still relies, unlike Britain and the United States, on a large number of independent bookshops rather than national or international chains; bookshops that function as local gathering places where readers have a personal relationship with the bookseller; where children feel at home and get to know what it is like to take a book from a shelf, read a little of this book or that, and choose what they want to take away.

These independent bookshops—Gleebooks or Constant Reader or Better Read than Dead in Sydney, Readings or

Hill of Content in Melbourne, Avid Reader in Brisbane, along with others all up and down the country—are also where writers of my sort, and Peter Carey or Helen Garner or Gerald Murnane, make most of their sales, as do the many local writers who rely on such local publishers as Text, Scribe, Black Inc., Giramondo and the university presses, who in this country publish poetry and fiction, biography and other forms of non-fiction as well as scholarly texts.

This mutually dependent world of publishers, booksellers and writers whose works may have both a local and an international life, is, as I said earlier, an unusually healthy one. It is also rich in variety and depth, but most of all it is rare. Australians are among the world's most dedicated readers, and have been since the 1830s (one-third of all books published in Britain in the nineteenth century went to Australia). So this book culture we are dealing with is long established, and many factors, not all of them understood, or even known, are essential to its survival. We should be very wary of disturbing it to serve some economic theory that has to do with cheaper books for the ordinary reader. It is the extraordinary reader we should be thinking of, who will not thank us for cheaper overseas publications if their local bookshops disappear, their local publishers can no longer compete, and what has become a rich publishing world goes back to being what it was in the 1950s, when fewer than a dozen novels were published each year in Australia and half that number of poetry collections, all from the same publisher.

All this is important to the national consciousness but also to the working lives of writers and booksellers in a place that, even in the digital age, remains isolated, and has, within the larger English-speaking world of Britain and the United States, a relatively small population. I offer, for what it is worth, an account of my own experience as a writer; one of many, each one unique but also typical.

I have, since my first collection of poems, *Bicycle*, in 1970, had only one publisher for poetry, the University of Queensland Press, which in 1975 also published my first novel, *Johnno*. When I found myself writing a second piece of fiction, a poetic monologue by the Roman poet Ovid, I simply put it away in a drawer, convinced that after the condescending, and sometimes hostile, reception of *Johnno*, no Australian publisher would be interested since it wasn't even 'one of our own stories'.

Quite by accident, Julie Strand, the wife of a visiting American poet, Mark Strand, asked if she could look at it, and a month later rang and asked if she could take the manuscript back to New York, where, it now emerged, she worked for a small but highly respected publisher, George Braziller. Within weeks Braziller had bought the book for US$1000 and advised me to get an agent. The book, *An Imaginary Life*, was published in mid-1978, but had by then made enough of a prepublication splash for Felicity Bryant, the London rep of my newly acquired agent, Curtis Brown, to get three offers from British publishers. Of these I chose Chatto & Windus, for no other reason than that they had been the publishers of Freud and Proust. But the choice was a lucky one. In the frenzy of international takeovers of the next decade, the other two publishers disappeared while Chatto went on to become part of Random Century, then Random House. When, in 1983, I made the only change of my publishing life, from Braziller to Pantheon (Knopf), I became a fully 'vertical' author with the same publisher in Britain, the United States, Canada and Australia.

Meanwhile, at the beginning of 1978, after Braziller's acceptance of *An Imaginary Life*, I had made another change. I had decided it was time to sit down quietly somewhere and find out what other books I might have in me, but somewhere away from the advisors and watchers I would have if I stayed in Australia. I gave up my job at Sydney University, cashed in my super ($8000) to buy a house in a remote village in southern Tuscany, and since I had no-one but myself who would suffer from the consequences, decided to live there on the rent from my Sydney apartment and whatever I could earn as a full-time writer.

Over the next six years I published three novels, a collection of stories, a 'memoir'—*12 Edmondstone Street*—and a third collection of poems. In this I was greatly aided by a 3-year fellowship from the Literature Board of the Australia Council (1979–81), that gave me time to establish, book by book, an Australian but also a British and North American readership.

Growing a readership, and maintaining it, but also the loyalty of a good publisher, is what keeps a writer's books in print. It is staying in print, the royalties from a back-list, along with translation rights, film rights, and here in Australia the Public Lending Right—the royalty from the number of books a writer has in public libraries—that has given me a sustainable living.

Essential to this are royalties; guaranteed originally for twenty-five, later seventy, years after the writer's death—which means, so long as a writer stays in print, for the whole of his or her lifetime and beyond.

I am simply flabbergasted by the suggestion that alone in Australia, with its smaller population and limited capacity for publication, the duration of copyright should be lowered, within the writer's lifetime, to fifteen years.

By this measure, after forty years of full-time work, of my nine novels and three collections of stories, only two would offer me continued financial support. I would, as an Australian writer, be dependent for my income only on the support of my non-Australian readers.

Monica McInerney

Long before I was a full-time writer, I was a full-time reader.

As a child growing up in rural South Australia, I read a diet of mostly English and American stories. I knew more about Mark Twain's Mississippi River and Enid Blyton's English woods and islands than I did about my own country. It felt rare and thrilling to find a story with Australian settings, characters and lives.

Times changed. To see the rich diet of Australian stories now available for children and adults is a marvellous thing. Australian stories are more than mirrors. They inform us, entertain us, give us pride in our country, teach us about Australian lives different than ours, challenge us, amuse us. They make us feel, we, as Australians, have a place in the world.

I feel that pride when I go into a bookshop in Dublin, or London, or Chicago, or Berlin and see Australian writers on the shelves. There are so many—Hannah Kent, Tim Winton, Kate Morton, Liane Moriarty, Garth Nix, Graeme Simsion, Richard Flanagan, Geraldine Brooks, Peter Carey, Thomas Keneally, among others. All are writers whose careers began in Australia and who now reach worldwide audiences, with their distinctly Australian voices.

All of these writers—and many more—were nurtured and published at home in Australia before they sold internationally. I am one of them. A publisher at Penguin Australia took a chance on me in 2000 with my first manuscript. It was clear to me from the beginning that my publisher was determined to help me as a writer, encourage me to develop my storytelling, to stay with me for the long haul.

Writing books takes time, imagination, discipline, self-belief and support. It is not a career that automatically delivers an instant salary or instant success. While I was writing my first three novels, I still needed to earn a wage in the 'real' world. After fifteen years of secure full-time jobs in marketing, tourism and children's television, I became a temp. I took short-term jobs that literally bought me writing time. I would temp for a month, write full-time for a few weeks, temp for another month. It was a risk I was willing to take, in the hope that a full-time writing career might become a reality.

I am one of the lucky ones. My Australian publisher put great support behind my first three books, promoting my stories, touring me, demonstrating at every step that they believed in my stories and believed that Australian readers would respond to them too. All three books became top ten bestsellers in Australia. By my fourth book, I was able to stop temping and write full-time.

Since then, I have written another eight novels, twelve in total, all of which have been bestsellers in Australia, been published internationally, been translated into more than a dozen languages, won and been shortlisted for awards. Those twelve books have not only allowed me to make a living as a full-time writer, but also created employment in Australia for editors, designers, marketing people, sales people, booksellers, distributors. I am still with the same publisher in Australia. I still have the same editor. It has been a long-term partnership.

I knew the team at Penguin Australia believed in me creatively, but I was also always fully aware that publishing is a business. They could be confident about building me as an author, backing my work, encouraging me to grow as a writer, because they had the security of robust copyright laws safeguarding their investment in me. Even as they celebrated in my publication and growing success in overseas markets, they knew that their customers—my readers in Australia—remained theirs. That confidence in investing in local authors will be one of the first casualties of a change in our territorial agreements.

If Australian publishers have no guarantee that they can sell their books competitively and fairly in their own market, why will they take a risk and nurture a new or young writer? Slowly, surely, fewer Australian stories will appear in Australian bookshops. It won't only be publishers and writers who lose out. So will Australian readers.

Since I was first published in Australia in 2001, I have received thousands of letters, emails and messages via social media from readers in Australia. If I was to summarise what the messages say, it would be this—my readers recognise themselves, their lives, their families in my stories, my characters, my settings. I write international family comedy–dramas, but always with an Australian setting, with Australian characters and from an Australian point of view. Several of my novels have been set in my own home town, Clare in South Australia. I have heard many stories of people visiting Clare after reading my books. I've also received messages from readers overseas who have become curious about Australia after reading my books, have planned visits there or gone on to read other Australian novels.

Books can be ambassadors. Books open up the world. They inform, entertain and console us as human beings. They remind us we are not alone in our fears, our problems, our hopes. They take us out of our own lives, introduce us to new places, new countries, new experiences. They connect us. They keep me connected to home. For family reasons, I move between Ireland and Australia, but a constant diet of Australian fiction and non-fiction keeps me informed, entertained, challenged and in touch with my home country.

Writing and publishing are not the same as selling food-stuffs, clothes or cars. What we create isn't a product made on a conveyor belt or by a machine. It is an object that exists because of a single spark of a writer's imagination, an idea that with time, patience and hard work—by an entire team of people—becomes a finished book. The irony is that a lack of imagination and lack of understanding about the value— financially and emotionally—of books in our cultural life is now endangering that same process.

I am an Australian writer. I am an Australian reader. I know the publishing industry from both sides. I know what it is worth creatively and financially. It's not too late to say no to these proposed changes. I urge Australian politicians to show faith in Australian storytellers, to show their support for our book industry. I ask every Australian book lover—readers, writers, booksellers, editors, publishers, designers, publicists, printers, sales reps, teachers, librarians—to stand up for Australian stories, to ask friends and family to sign the BooksCreateAustralia petition and to help keep our stories alive.

Alex Miller

The Coalition Government has rightly made much recently of its policy to promote growth and jobs through its support of small and medium-size Australian businesses. The Australian publishing industry is made up of hundreds of small and medium-sized businesses. The independent Australian publishing industry, on which printers and allied trades also rely for much of their work, directly and indirectly employs thousands of skilled and professional workers. Abolishing territorial copyright would place Australian publishing at an impossible business disadvantage in relation to its overseas competitors. Some publishers would almost certainly be driven to the wall. An essential of any modern civilised nation is a robust independent publishing industry which can offer to the reading public the stories of its writers. The cultural independence and richness of any nation depends on the writers who tell the stories of that nation.

My own writing took many years, indeed decades, to mature before it began to earn me an income on which I could live and support a family. My writing has been a life-long meditation on Australia and our people, our origins and experiences, our tragedies and our triumphs. My work has been inspired by the lives of loved ones and friends, some of whom have been Indigenous people, such as Bo Rennie in *Journey to the Stone Country*, and Dougald Gnapun and his children in *Landscape of Farewell*. All lifelong friends. These stories are uniquely Australian, they belong to all of us, they speak our peculiar tones and reflect our social conditions and the peculiarities of our history and our regional differences. All of them have been translated and published overseas as well as here, and have carried with them the face and the voice of our uniquely Australian culture and its complexities. No-one else is going to write these stories but us, Australian writers. We can only write what we know and have lived. If territorial copyright is abandoned, Australian writers, and with them our stories, will cease to be supported and we will become a country that is silent about itself. My publishers, Allen & Unwin, are an independent Australian small business. They keep all my books in print here and in the United Kingdom. Through them my voice and the voice of Australian storytelling is heard here and around the world. In New Zealand, where territorial copyright was abolished, domestic publishing has been killed and with it the voice of New Zealand storytelling. The same will happen here if the Coalition carries through its threat to abolish territorial copyright. Australia will be left without a vigorous and unique voice at home and in the wider world. Our stories will not survive. No-one will tell them.

No other countries, except New Zealand and Hong Kong, have hamstrung the growth and employment potential of their publishing industry and threatened the voice of their storytellers by abolishing territorial copyright. If the Australian Government's proposal to abolish territorial copyright is carried through, Australia will become a client nation to the London- and New York-based multinational publishing corporations, and will be uniquely handicapped in this regard, here and overseas. Coming from the Coalition Government, the abolition of territorial copyright must be a policy that is impossible for voters to understand or for which they are able to have any sympathy. It will be a policy that is universally condemned by the millions of Australian readers who stand to lose the unique voice of their own culture.

It is already difficult for Australian writers to make a good living from writing. If territorial copyright is abolished their incomes will be further reduced and their position marginalised. Such a policy, if carried through, would seriously inhibit the richness and diversity of Australia's cultural community. The importance to any country of the vigour of its cultural community was memorably expressed by Winston Churchill during Britain's most perilous time in the Second World War. Churchill's cabinet was desperate to increase available funds for munitions and armaments and it was suggested to Churchill he cut the arts budget. His response to this was, '*But that is what we are fighting for*'.

Nothing less than Australia's cultural independence is at stake in this. I am not alone in believing the hard-won cultural independence of this nation to be something worth fighting for and, if necessary, dying for. Once a country's cultural independence has been seriously eroded and undermined, as it will be if territorial copyright is abolished, an entire generation of insight and historic perception of society is lost. Such a loss is not recoverable. There will be no going back and recovering what has been forfeited. No democratic government, I suggest, has the right to so endanger the cultural vigour of its own country, and any government that does so will be remembered in history for having done irreparable harm to the community whose care was given into its charge by the voters.

To abolish territorial copyright in the twenty-first century will be viewed by all who hear of it as a short-sighted and reactionary, not to say cruel and unjustified, policy. Small business and jobs growth, as well as the voice of our writers, can only be inhibited by such a policy. The only winners will be the already far too powerful multinational conglomerates based in New York and London. These powerful conglomerates have no interest in Australian nation building. To abolish territorial copyright is not only against the interests of Australians generally but runs counter to the repeatedly stated aims of the Coalition Government. Writers and publishers will be sure to educate the Australian public on the harm this policy will be certain to wreak on all of us.

If this policy is implemented, that will not be the end of the matter. Writers and publishers will continue to stand up and speak loudly against it and will not cease their opposition to it until it is repealed by a future government. It is a policy that makes no sense at all to Australians and is a serious threat to our independence.

I ask the government to reconsider the proposal to abolish territorial copyright, if not because of something said by an Australian writer or publisher, then through a moment's reflection on the vision of Britain's greatest prime minister, when he claimed it was Britain's and Europe's cultural freedom and independence that they were fighting to preserve during the Second World War. No less than this is at stake here today. A nation should be proud of its independent publishing industry and should do everything in its power to preserve and encourage it, and the writers it supports. No country can claim to be a nation if it does not tell its own stories. All civilised peoples know this. Without writers and publishers, small nations soon become mere clients of their more powerful trading partners. A vigorous and independent culture is an essential part of every nation's identity.

Frank Moorhouse

To: Malcolm, Bill,

Cc: Queen Elizabeth, Head of State (you may remember me, you have given me a couple of medals and I met your late sister, Margaret), Richard Di Natale, leader Australian Greens (we haven't met), Barnaby Joyce and all Independents

Re: KPIs—'Things is crook in Tallarook and there's no dough in Dubbo ...' (Jack O'Hagan)

Dear Malcolm,
we have dined together at the Catalina, and you are my local member, so we see each other around the neighbourhood, but I haven't had a chance to talk with you about the KPIs.

Dear Bill,
we have not met, but I have been a union organiser, and I edited *The Australian Worker* for the AWU, your former union, so we share some common background.

I thought I would take the unusual step as a writer to email you as a matter of urgency, about the national culture ... and the state of the arts and intellectual life in this country ... and thought I would give you our latest Key Performance Indicators.

Seriously, over these last months I have received letters requesting my support from people and organisations who are deeply alarmed at the decline of political recognition and funding for the arts, including writing, publishing, scholarship, the ABC—that is, the community of arts and ideas—what was once known as Science and Letters or longhairs.

Because of changes to the taxation act the art market, including Indigenous art, has plummeted, undermining the economy of painting and sculpture.

There is a feeling that in recent years there has been a rather steep devaluation of our national culture—more a degrading of it—by the withdrawal of funding: from the Australia Council (reduced by $104.8 million), the Australian Research Council (reduced by $86 million), CSIRO (reduced by $111 million), the ABC (reduced by $254 million), Screen Australia (reduced by $38 million), not to forget the National Library, the National Museum, the National Gallery, the National Portrait Gallery, the Museum of Australian Democracy, and the National Film and Sound Archive, all of which have lost funding. Literary magazines such as *Meanjin* (been around for seventy-five years), *Quadrant, Island* and *Sleepers*, and sixty-two performance groups have lost funding, and maybe their existence, because of the cuts to the Australia Council. As for what is happening in the universities, as an example, the ANU has lost fifteen staff from its Asian Studies centre because of budget cuts.

There has been a failure to address the slow collapse of print newspapers and a failure to see the profession of journalism as being a Public Good and to find ways of preserving quality journalism through, say, statutory corporations or foundations—at least until we are sure of what is happening with print and the Internet.

They are a crucial part of the intellectual life of this country. The Australian Computer Society argues that the reach, speed and quality of a national broadband network (NBN) is now an integral part of a contemporary creative economy. Australia, one of the richest countries, currently ranks poorly in this area—sixtieth in the world for internet speed and download capacity despite an accelerated NBN rollout in recent years.

The rug is being pulled out from under the arts and intellectual life, making it difficult for many to maintain a decent life and to embark on creative and intellectual enterprises. We are being dumbed down—or more, in the minds of some politicians, *shut up*, buried.

Such wide expression of grave alarm for the national culture at a federal election has not happened before in my lifetime and I reckon I have consciously followed about twenty federal elections.

The mission of every federal government is to raise revenue to meet the standards of public service expected by the electorate, to meet expectations of fairness, and to serve cultural enrichment which in turn helps create a responsive and vibrant society—determined by judgement, vision and even faith (by faith I mean that in the absence of 'metrics' we sometimes choose to believe that this is the best way forward).

A metric: public social spending (for the vulnerable), excluding health, as a percentage of GDP is in Denmark 24 per cent and in Australia 12 per cent.

Maybe it might be easier for some in government to understand what I am talking about if I use the Key Performance Indicators asked of the community of arts and ideas by government funding agencies.

A few mates helped me with it and they have signed off on this KPI acquittal (except one, see below) and we had a problem with the metrics.

Key Performance Indicators

Evidence of economic, environmental, social, health and/ or cultural benefits to Australia arising from the practice of the arts and research: More than 95 per cent of completed arts and research projects would report that their objectives were met, well, in the arts, give or take 50 per cent and fingers crossed (and if not, the applicants told me that they would try harder next time—things do not always work out as you want them to in the arts). Yes, the arts and intellectual research do '*build social and economic capital*'—the 2008-09 National Accounts puts the cultural and creative input to the economy as double agriculture, forestry and fishing; a couple of points behind construction; and bigger than education and training. However, despite what it 'does for the nation', it doesn't do much for the building of personal economies for artists and thinkers. As well, artists and thinkers '*drive innovation*', in fact, we do little else other than 'drive innovation' all our lives. And, yes, we think that we probably '*promote social inclusion by bridging communica-tions between disparate groups*', assuming that the disparate groups wish to be communicated and bridged—sometimes we have to push it down their throats. Oh yes, the community of ideas and arts also '*works to counter disaffection through alienation*', even when they themselves are feeling rather disaffected and have always, through the centuries, often felt alienated, although it has been demonstrated that a decent income for those working in the community of arts and ideas could allay some alienation and disaffection quite quickly.

Evidence of the building of Australia's imaginative and intellectual capacity through the winning of prizes and awards: There is excellent evidence that arts and intellectual projects win prestigious prizes and awards, here and internationally. (But, strangely, some of those works which do not win prizes sometimes have a longer life than the prize winners and are ultimately considered to be of more importance. Even those projects which do not win prizes are often valued highly. Odd.)

Evidence of the building of Australia's imaginative and intellectual capacity through the winning of audiences and readership: Yes, we have won ever-larger audiences and readerships—at least, sometimes, sometimes not, sometimes no-one turns up except friends and family, sometimes the audience does not appear until fifty to 100 years later. Any suggestions?

Building Australia's imaginative capacity by giving early-career training: Great evidence exists that established artists and thinkers support 'career opportunities for early-career artists'. It has to be said that early-career artists and thinkers can be very difficult to work with because they believe they know best: established artists and thinkers—and early-career artists and thinkers—can also fall into romantic illusions and delightfully errant fantasy when working together. Nothing much can be done about this. By the way, career is a word we don't use much in the arts—maybe 'obsession' or 'commitment', actually, without going into it here, the artist and the thinker and the society are part of a 'gift economy', as well as the market economy. The gift economy is constructed on the implied invitation from the society to writers and thinkers to present, to offer, say, an original work of art, new thinking, to the society, first as a gift. The obligation of the society then is to respond, to receive the work or reject it, and, if accepted and used, there arises the third part of the formula—the obligation of the community to adequately reward the artist for their initial gift and to encourage them in further creative and intellectual ventures (e.g. patronage).

Building Australia's imaginative capacity—creation in areas of national priority: I can supply evidence that arts and intellectual research projects address all areas of 'national priority' (in so far as these exist in any coherent way), and, more, even by dreaming up some of those priorities and by establishing yet other stranger 'areas of priority' neither national nor recognisable or expected, and even by demolishing some 'national priorities' by ridicule. Can't do much about this.

Further, in reply to the KPIs' terms of reference, other broader evidence is provided in an Overview of Western Civilisation—but only since the Renaissance (to be forwarded). Also to be forwarded are statements made by Winston Churchill (beginning with ... *The State owes it to itself to sustain and encourage [arts] ... Ill fares the race which fails to salute the arts with the reverence and delight which are their due*), Robert Menzies (beginning with ... *We are so little concerned with the things that really make life worth living that we ... expect many of our best writers and artists to live in a sort of eccentric penury*), Gough Whitlam (beginning with ... *To help cultivate a rich and enduring national pride, and to enlarge the people's opportunities for cultural fulfilment, we have given high priority to the encouragement of the arts*) and Malcolm Fraser, (beginning with '... *These people looking for efficiencies have no understanding that governments have to do things you can't put a dollar on...*').

The KPI is signed off by The Man from Snowy River, who said he can't answer the KPI more fully because the colt from old Regret has got away.

Dorothea Mackellar, aged eighteen, also signed off on the KPI and asked me to say that she also loves

> ... a sunburnt country,
> A land of sweeping plains,
> Of ragged mountain ranges,
> Of droughts and flooding rains.
> I love her far horizons,
> I love her jewel-sea,
> Her beauty and her terror—
> The wide brown land for me!

Henry Lawson was indisposed but asked me to say as an addition to the KPI,

... my ways are strange ways and new ways and old ways,
And deep ways and steep ways and high ways and low;
I'm at home and at ease on a track that I know not,
And restless and lost on a road that I know.

I tried to get Clancy of the Overflow to sign off on the KPI—but that didn't work out, either.

I had written him a letter which I had, for want of better
Knowledge, sent to where I met him down the Lachlan,
years ago,
He was shearing when I knew him, so I sent the letter to him,
Just 'on spec', addressed as follows, 'Clancy, of The Overflow'.

And an answer came directed in a writing unexpected,
(And I think the same was written with a thumb-nail dipped
in tar)
'Twas his shearing mate who wrote it, and *verbatim* I will
quote it:
'Clancy's gone to Queensland droving, and we don't know
where he are.'

Matthew Reilly

We Wouldn't Do It to Our Olympians, So Why Do It to Our Authors and Publishers?

Imagine if it was announced that the Australian Olympic swimming team will now include swimmers *who are not Australian*.

On top of that, imagine if team members would now be selected by *British* and *American* coaches based in London and New York.

It would cause uproar.

Yet, this is exactly what is about to happen to Australian authors and publishers.

Writing and publishing books is not an Olympic sport. If it were, Australian writers and publishers would be winning as many gold medals as our swim team—in the world of publishing, we punch way above our weight for a relatively small country.

Recently, the Australian Government's Productivity Commission suggested removing territorial copyright protections for Australian authors and publishers.

This is insanity.

It's economic insanity. It's cultural insanity.

It would hand control of our strong local publishing industry to publishing houses in London and New York (at a time when the United States and United Kingdom have no inclination to similarly open their markets). Just as with the swim team example, some authors like me will be okay—I'm sure my overseas publishers would love to storm the Australian market with their editions of my books, the market that discovered me and nurtured my early career—but most local authors will be shut out.

If writing books was an Olympic sport, we'd have a world-beating team: Morrissey, Griffiths, Zusak, Moriarty, Winton, Keneally, Flanagan, Morton and maybe even me.

Like many of those authors, I got my start as an author because of our world-class local publishing industry. If we give away the keys to the kingdom, who will find new Australian authors?

It's the job of the Australian Government to promote strong local industries, not destroy them. Like I said, this is madness.

We wouldn't do this to our Olympic swimmers. So why do it to our world-class authors and publishers?

Michael Robotham

Nobody's Land

Australian authors tend to be gentle folk who spend their time in lonely garrets and garden sheds rather than fronting protest campaigns or carrying placards. We let our stories speak for us, creating worlds and characters that come to life in a reader's imagination, revealing truths, touching hearts and maybe, if we're very lucky, changing someone's life.

So when these same writers emerge from their self-imposed exile to campaign so vociferously against a sitting government on Twitter, Facebook and in the mainstream media, you can be sure the issue is of the upmost importance to Australian readers. When the winners of four Booker Prizes between them—Peter Carey, Tom Keneally and Richard Flanagan—write an open letter to the government trying to save Australian stories and storytelling, every Australian should take note.

The reason is simple. The rather bizarrely named Productivity Commission has recommended radical changes to

Australia's intellectual property laws and copyright, which will silence Australian voices, shrink our vibrant local publishing industry and adversely affect local writers, publishers, booksellers, readers and, in particular, our culture.

In a nutshell (because others have explained it more succinctly in these pages) the government plans to remove Australia's territorial copyright and water down our intellectual property laws because it believes the current system stifles innovation and makes books more expensive. The Productivity Commission's draft report doesn't offer any evidence to support this premise, relying instead on dry economic arguments about protectionism and open markets.

What it completely fails to appreciate—but every reader knows passionately—is that books are not widgets. Books are not sweatshop T-shirts, or used cars, or the latest software or a pharmaceutical. Books are part of our culture. They tell our stories. They connect Australians with their past and with each other; they 'export' Australian ideas and ideals to the outside world.

The Productivity Commission doesn't seem to like books. Even worse, it thinks Australian writers are wasting our time and talents and should be doing something more efficient. The solution is to remove the copyright protections that safeguard authors' incomes.

Parallel importation rules (PIRs) are the market mechanism that allows Australians to compete with other English-language writers and publishers throughout the world. By having different copyright territories around the world, an author can sell his or her rights to foreign publishers, knowing that the work is well published, royalties are collected and his or her story finds a wider audience.

These rules are not a hidden subsidy to the publishing industry or a form of protectionism. They exist almost everywhere in the world.

But now the Productivity Commission (that name always makes me laugh) wants to abolish PIRs by the end of 2017. In effect, Australia will become a publishing *terra nullius* (nobody's land)—an open market, to be exploited and pillaged by foreign publishers and wholesalers.

The last time Australia was deemed *terra nullius* we became the dumping ground for Britain's unwashed and unwanted. This time we will be flooded by bestselling books, published and printed overseas, as well as being swamped by unloved books, surplus stock, added print runs and second-rate novels from the United Kingdom, United States and Canada.

Normally I'm all for a level playing field. I don't like protectionism because it diminishes competition, but this has nothing to do with fairness. In practice, the British and Americans are not going to open up their borders and allow Australian publishers to ship books into the United Kingdom and United States. Why not? Because they protect and nurture their writers and they are essentially net exporters of copyright. Only in Australia do we consider treating writers with such disdain—telling them to 'get a proper job'.

I'm going to talk about me now. I wanted to be a writer from the age of twelve and spent decades honing my craft, first as a journalist and then as a ghostwriter. My first novel triggered a bidding war at the London Book Fair in 2002 and has since been translated into twenty-three languages.

I am one of the lucky few. The oft-quoted figure for earnings of Australian authors is $12 900 a year, but I make a decent living out of this, while better writers than me struggle to make a living, hoping for a breakthrough.

The changes to Australia's territorial copyright will adversely affect my income, but I'm not trying to 'protect my patch' or safeguard my earnings. I fight this fight for the next generation of Australian writers and those who are still struggling to find a readership.

For an established author like myself the removal of the existing PIRs will mean that UK and US editions of my books can be sold on the same shelves as my Australian edition. My US editions have different spellings and, in the past, have had entire chapters either added or removed. I do not want these versions turning up in Australia. I will receive a smaller royalty on these books or no royalty at all if they are dumped by a US or UK wholesaler who has picked up remaindered stock or oversupply.

The Productivity Commission has argued that this surplus stock only occurs due to an author's 'failure in another market'. This is simply wrong. Publishers are always looking for new markets. Almost inevitably, print runs in the United States and United Kingdom will become larger to accommodate a new territory that is opening up. Australia will again be *terra nullius*.

My Australian publishers won't have the same opportunity to sell my Australian edition in the United States or United Kingdom or Europe because these markets are protected, either by law or in practice. So much for a level playing field.

It is well known that publishers rely on the success of a relative handful of bestselling books each year to fund new authors, nurture writers and publish uniquely

Australian stories. Many of these bestsellers are by recognised authors. If we surrender territorial copyright, anyone will be able to ship these titles into Australia, undercutting the local product being offered by local publishers.

Our publishing industry will shrink, something the Productivity Commission actually acknowledges in the draft recommendations, but it says that's okay, because books *may* be cheaper. When the industry shrinks, fewer Australian authors will be published. Advances will shrink, marketing budgets will dry up and money won't be available to help writers tour, or to promote their books to Australian readers and to the world.

There will be other effects. Usually local authors rely on local publishers to find international markets for their books. However, once we surrender our territorial copyright, these same publishers will surely think long and hard about whether they offer a brilliant new novel to a US or UK publisher. To do so would risk having copies sent straight back into Australia, competing with the local product because we will be *terra nullius*.

Can an author stop this? No.

Can he or she put it in a contract to prevent it happening? No.

Will their books be dumped in Australia? Yes.

Will they earn less money? Yes.

Will their advances shrink? Yes.

Will fewer Australian writers be published? Yes.

Will books be cheaper? Nobody knows.

The people arguing for these changes are a few large book retailers and the usual economic rationalists who have never created intellectual property that might be worth valuing or protecting. In opposition to the changes, speaking as one, are Australia's authors, publishers, printers and the Australian Booksellers Association. A $2.2 billion industry that employs over twenty thousand people and is one of Australia's greatest cultural success stories is united in condemning the changes.

Those few retailers who are fighting for the removal of PIRs will, I'm certain, come to regret the removal of territorial copyright (as they have in New Zealand). I envision a future where pop-up shops and two-dollar stores will turn up on Australian high streets selling thousands of purposely over-printed, remaindered, surplus and predominantly second-rate books written by US and UK authors. Proper bookstores will disappear and important Australian stories will be swamped by a tsunami of mediocrity.

How is this beneficial? Surely it will lead further to the McDonaldisation of our society and the eroding of our cultural identity.

In addition to the changes in PIRs, the Productivity Commission thinks Australia would be better off without copyright, recommending that we adopt a watered-down US version that is ironically called 'fair use', but could be called 'free use'. Similar laws were adopted in Canada in 2012, resulting in schools, universities and companies being able to photocopy millions of pages from books and journals without permission or payment, undermining the livelihood of authors and publishers. Writers have lost precious income and publishers have withdrawn from the market completely or cut back on the number of books they commission.

How is it desirable for those who have the talent to create something, be it words, music, images or whatever, to be deprived of the right to profit from that talent? And anyone who asserts that films, music and books of the same quantity or quality will continue to be produced if we had no copyright is talking nonsense. It would lead to a world where writing, filmmaking, photography, journalism and song-writing would be forever hobbies, never careers. Either that or we will regress to a situation where artists survive thanks to patronage and political favours, going cap-in-hand to governments, corporations or the elites.

The Productivity Commission favours this outcome. Government should pay for culture, it believes, recommending that arts funding be increased to compensate for loss of income. Yes, *increased*—that's not a misprint. Given the slashing of arts funding in the past three years, I would laugh if I weren't weeping.

I'm only going to touch upon the Productivity Commission's other stated belief that the optimal copyright term should be closer to fifteen to twenty-five years after creation, considerably less than seventy years after death. On that basis, my first novel, *The Suspect,* will be out of copyright two years from now. Movies can be made, TV shows filmed and multiple versions published—making money for everyone except me.

Again, I could weep.

None of these proposed changes are about greater competition or cheaper books and they have nothing to do with creating a level playing field. Adopting the Productivity Commission's draft recommendations will mean asking Australian writers and publishers to run uphill, into the wind, against twenty-three players with a dodgy referee and a rigged result. Even worse, we will become mere spectators, not even in the game.

Australian writers care about this. You have read and enjoyed our stories; now hear our voices. We need your help. Join the fight and show this government that Australia is not a publishing *terra nullius*. It belongs to Australians.

Magda Szubanski
Creating Australia

I had no idea how hard it is to write a book. The sheer slog of it. The years of grinding psychological, even physical, labour. Sat hunched over a laptop for hours every day until your fingers cramp and your neck feels like someone has tried to drill a rusty nail through your vertebrae.

And then there is the emotional cost. Some sentences in *Reckoning* were like pulling strands of razor wire from the soft flesh of my heart. After doing some of the research—learning about the Holocaust, watching footage of my father talking about it, re-reading his letters, poring like a scholarship student over history books about the First and Second World Wars, reading current literature about post-traumatic stress disorder (PTSD)—I would have to lie down for days, teetering on the brink of a reactive depression. Sometimes tipping over. I lost months of sleep, agonising about how to depict hell without hurting anyone, causing offence or writing a tome so miserable no-one would want to read it.

And I had to feel the feelings again. In order to describe it, I had to relive being a suicidal teenager realising she was gay in a world that despised her. I don't want to bleat or whinge. But that was not easy.

But the art of the artist is to make it look easy. You don't want anyone to see the grunt work. The illusion of Fred Astaire dancing on air would be ruined if we saw the hours, months, years of rehearsal. We are like children who still want to believe in magic. No-one wants to see the blood, sweat and tears.

* * *

For eight long years, that is what I did. And was it worth it? Of course it was.

Every single day now I get letters, emails, tweets from people telling me how they laughed and wept while reading my book. How it has changed their perspective and given them the words to understand what they are going through. How it has made them feel less alone. People stop me in the street, in cafés, in theatres, in supermarkets, grabbing my arm, fixing me with a look—determined to connect.

I have been in the public eye for thirty-two years. I am very well accustomed to being recognised, hugged, often kissed on the footpath. But nothing quite like this has ever happened to me before. Not with this ferocity and intensity. And that particular kind of cracked-wide-open-heartedness that only happens when sorrows are shared and we are busted down to the bare bones of who we really are. Why?

When you write a book, you hope to bring to the surface a truth that lies just below conscious awareness. To tell a story that is waiting to be told. *Reckoning* could not have been written anywhere else by anyone else. No-one else would have even known that this story existed. The waters of history would have closed over the courage and compassion of my Polish family, the Job-like suffering and dogged endurance of my Irish grandfather.

But deeper than that is the story of family, of the sins of the father, of broken people stumbling forward, loving the best they can in the only way they know how. It is a universal story. But it is also a uniquely Australian one. At heart, it is the story of how we all came to this country, at one time or another, fleeing the horrors of Europe and praying for a better life. This country, the vast, flat expanse of red dirt at the bottom of the world that carried all our dreams and fervid imaginings. Fresh air and wide-open spaces that dissolve and dissipate memory. Where, even if we never find it ourselves, our children or our children's children might find prosperity and redemption.

It is thought unseemly in this country to boast. But journeys to America have taught me that our national sport of self-deprecation is often just low self-esteem and envy dressed up as mateship and egalitarianism. This is a moment when we need to defend and take pride in our culture and our work. It is important that you know that I did not just pull this book out of my arse. It is not the first thing I have ever written. I have spent the last three and a half decades communicating with the public. Honing my skills, listening, polishing, perfecting every sentence and word. In films, on television, in advertisements, on stage and in public appearances I have weighed and calibrated meaning. In other words, I am by now an experienced professional.

Still. Writing a book is something else again. I found a truth in writing that would have been impossible for me to uncover in any other form. The give and take, the push and pull, the compromise of everyday exchange can silence truth. Shy, gentle truths lose their confidence in the rough and tumble. Conformity dictates. I'm not strong enough to resist the pressure to fit in. In the seclusion of my study I could follow the stream of consciousness to unexpected destinations. I could arrive at long-buried feelings and experiences that lie at the heart of us all. An outrider, I could find the lone truths that wander the boundaries. And I could bring them back and add my little strand of meaning to the web of communication that binds us.

* * *

I love popular culture. God knows I have spent most of my life and made my livelihood there. But much instant, popular culture is a thinly disguised vehicle for selling what will ultimately become landfill. It is like an endless feedback loop, a creative *Groundhog Day*. It regurgitates, repackages and resells what we already believe about ourselves. It reflects back to us who we are but what it does not do is show us who we might be. That kind of imagination takes time and patience. It takes deep reflection and contemplation.

The current proposed changes to copyright law are being suggested to us in the name of greater 'freedom'. The assumption is that relaxing the rules that govern the book market will generate ideas, 'open things up'. But the real, profit-driven motive is to create an alliance between multinational corporations and consumers and drive a wedge between consumers and creators. Creators are somehow now the enemy. Pesky creators are the fly in the ointment, driving up prices and demanding to be paid for their work. It serves the profiteer's argument to depict creators as replaceable amateurs.

Even though the creators are actually us. Many of us are, or aspire to be, creators of some description. Whether that be as a writer of fiction, textbooks, advertisements, songs, self-help books, family history or trade manuals. Or perhaps we wish such a future for our children. The high-minded rhetoric of collectivism and cooperation has been appropriated by the skimmers and scammers. In other words, we 'share' but they profit. In my view this will not open up a cornucopia of ideas. The opposite will happen. People will become tight-fisted and circumspect with their ideas and knowledge. Robber baron corporations are selling us a culture of theft. Private property—once the very solid foundation on which free-market capitalism was built—has become a fluid concept, increasingly open to interpretation and dispute. Its boundaries have been made porous. Vested corporate interests fan the flames of a narcissistic sense of entitlement. Even the word 'piracy', with its seductive Johnny Depp overtones, makes stealing cool. But don't you dare try and steal the corporation's stuff! Just stick to stealing from one another please. In the digital universe we are creating, our young people, that beautiful new genera-tion of thinkers and creators, will become the intellectual equivalent of textile workers—offshore outworkers who make cat videos in exchange for their three minutes of fame (fifteen minutes was so last century). And the young, because they're not old enough to know better, will collude in their own destruction.

Why does all of this matter anyway?

Because we are not born knowing how to be in the world. Our culture teaches us how to be human.

I was not born in this country. This country is not the place of my dreaming. The tales of my ancestors are of ice and snow and banishment to Siberia. Cautionary tales against the high price of idealism.

I wasn't born an Australian. I became one. Australian-ness was something I had to learn. And I can remember how it happened.

I was maybe nine or so. I was sitting in the classroom of my dusty, bush primary school. And the teacher gave us a story to read from an anthology of Australian literature. It was Henry Lawson—*The Drover's Wife*.

It is one of the most dramatic, pure tales of human survival I have ever encountered. The drover has been gone for six months. The Wife is left alone in the outback with her four children. There is not another soul for twenty miles. The scrappy house is full of cracks and gaps. A storm is approaching. And then a deadly black snake appears and takes up residence under the house.

Even sitting in my study now, just thinking about that story, my throat constricts and strange melancholy tears for a history that is not even mine press against the back of my eyes. I am there, with the Drover's Wife, alone in the unkind wilderness. I can feel the relentless expanse, the indifferent monotony of the Bush. Lawson's spare, unsentimental descriptions of this woman's profound loneliness and isolation pierce my heart. I can hear the slither of the black snake beneath the house. I can feel its sinister intent.

As I sat at my little wooden desk a century later reading the book, I understood viscerally what it took to build this country. What it means to be Australian. A white Australian, anyway.

And I would never have known that, had Lawson not trekked from Hungerford to Bourke, had he not watched and listened and learned and then written the story to tell it to a classroom full of children whose faces and names were undreamed of when he lived. And had a book not been published to preserve it.

Decades later I found it hard to read some of Kate Grenville's *The Secret River*. Despair relieved only by the elegiac beauty of her writing. With meticulous charity Grenville dragged me into the hollow belly of poverty-stricken London. Through her words I felt the raw ache of hunger and the bone-snapping cold. Her novel triggered race memories of my own family and my grandfather's ten dead siblings buried in the cold Irish earth. And the harrowing, inexorable conclusion confirmed my sense of the working-out of trauma, of the ways in which the brutalised in turn brutalise. And of how silences and quarter-acre blocks and the relentless pursuit of unimpeded views of coastline are used to occlude history and bury shame in this dangerous paradise.

When I studied it at university, Christina Stead's *The Man Who Loved Children* sharpened my ear to the private language of families. And, although the novel is set in Washington, we all knew it was really Stead's family, an Aussie family. And I felt a strange thrill of recognition to see a family as damaged and dangerous as my own; a family that used words as weapons in the battleground of psychological warfare.

Les Murray autopsied the brutal truth that I never dared let pass—the eroticide of the fat and ugly by the 'beautiful Nazis'. His frank, scarifying admissions allowed me to grieve and allowed me to be braver about my own shames and humiliations.

And in *Dead Europe,* the bare-knuckled courage with which Christos Tsiolkas stared down the demons of Greek anti-Semitism gave me the guts to walk into the minefield of Polish Catholic–Jewish relations.

Their writing exists within mine like a secret harmonic. At first glance you might not know it is there, but it is. Like a cultural trickle-down effect, it is present in all of my work, from *Reckoning* to *Big Girl's Blouse* to *Dogwoman*. And in the melancholy, indomitable, dogged optimism of Sharon Strzelecki there is something of the iconic Aussie spirit. Of the Drover's Wife.

My book does not exist in isolation. It is a conversation, a response to other books, other writers. As I read I am stimulated and provoked. Each author's thoughts and ideas land in my mind with a thud, sending my own thoughts scurrying in a thousand different directions. And I have no choice but to chase after those thoughts, to run them down, catch them and get them down on paper. I become part of a cultural chain reaction. That conversation is informed and safeguarded by copyright, the lever for reward that encourages every creator to write. And to dream.

Christos Tsiolkas
Hear Our Stories

At the dawn of the new millennium, as the music industry was collapsing from the havoc wreaked by emerging digital distribution and production platforms, I experienced schadenfreude. I know I wasn't alone. The industry had been treating music lovers abysmally for years, grossly inflating the prices of CDs and overseeing a sclerotic distribution network for both local and international music. Many of us also knew that the industry was venal when it came to the exploitation of the musicians. I have friends who found some success as music artists but that meant they were locked into contracts that in some cases see them still having to pay off accumulated debts from advances and tours accrued years, even decades, ago. For many of the musicians I know, the new digital era has allowed them to have a level of control and ownership of their artistic work that was inconceivable when they were dependent on distribution through the record companies. It is still hard for musicians, as it is for any artist, to make money from their craft. Spotify and iTunes are certainly not altruistic enablers of art: they too are powerful organisations in it for the money. But now that you can upload your work on a site such as Bandcamp, that you can produce your own video clip and place it on YouTube, musicians aren't saddled with the exorbitant debts of the past.

The Australian publishing industry is historically very different from the music industry and I think this is one of the key reasons why so many Australian writers have come out in opposition to the removal of the parallel importation rules (PIRs). Of course, one of the factors for our concern is monetary. I know that I am fortunate to live as a writer in Australia and I know that this is all too rare. But economic security did not come my way until my mid-forties and my support of PIRs predates the commercial success I had with my novel *The Slap*. Before that, I worked part-time at odd jobs for my livelihood while I concentrated on my vocation as a writer. My work was facilitated by my publishers, my editors, the international rights departments, the administrative staff, the marketing personnel and the women and men who went out to booksellers and passionately advocated for my writing. It may be that the recommendations suggested by the Productivity Commission will adversely affect my earnings as a writer. They may not. But what I do firmly believe is that they place the Australian publishing industry as an industry at risk. This is the danger that concerns me most: that the people who supported me as an emerging writer will lose *their* livelihood. And when we lose them, that support that we Australian writers depend on will also be gone.

The rationalists of economic liberalism do not differentiate between consumer products. At their most extreme they see no difference between the market for laundry detergent and the market for books. On the other side of the economic looking glass, there are ideologues of the left who identify every commercial and corporate entity as an enemy of true creative freedom and endeavour. My experience in the publishing world has given me a clear insight into how publishers operate and the truth is that almost without exception the women and men I have worked with are committed to books and to the importance of literature. There is a bottom line. There has to be. But one of the experiences I have most appreciated in being part of the Australian writing community is the collegiate goodwill that different publishers and workers in the industry have extended towards me. We meet over a drink at a writers' festival and we discuss books. We talk ideas and we constantly ask each other, What have you read recently? What have you loved? The publishers will sign the celebrity to make money but what they want most is to publish a writer whose voice hasn't yet been heard and should be heard. Unlike the music industry, I have never been asked to pay back an advance for a book that failed commercially. There is always an element of negotiation over money, and sometimes that can be difficult and uncomfortable. But I have tried to maintain the long view from the beginning: goodwill and passion alone don't pay for the editing, production and distribution of books. The publishers want to sell books, but I know what they want most is to publish books they love from writers they respect.

I am referring to relationships of trust and loyalty that cannot be captured in the dry rhetoric of economic papers. In the main, historically and to the present day, Australian publishing is marked by this care and prioritising of the importance of the Australian voice. Such relationships do depend on a shared vocabulary and the ineffable glue of mutual cultural understanding. It is my desire that we Australian writers work towards a language and expression that is firmly our own, that we help create an Australian English that is influenced by writing across the world but also unmistakeably sings in our voices and in our accents. There isn't some kind of template for what this writing might be. It encompasses the stories-within-stories that mark Alexis Wright's novels. I hear it in the urban Sydney chant that is Kate Grenville's *Lilian's Story* and the beautiful and vital coarseness of Malcolm Knox's *The Life*. I hear another Australia in Tim Winton and another in Richard Flanagan and yet another in Charlotte Wood. All of these writers have been championed by publishers who understood the importance of the stories they were telling, and the importance of the way they were telling those stories. In Emily Bitto's *The Strays*, a wonderful novel published two years ago by the independent publisher Affirm Press, we are reminded of the yearnings and aspirations of a previous generation of artists, and thus we are reminded of what we owe those previous generations. Would a non-Australian publisher have caught the nuances? Would they have thought them worth encouraging? A good publisher, wherever in the world they find themselves, will recognise good writing and a good story. But they are more attuned to the culture they come from. The Australian publisher works as a conduit to the greater world and they are the ones demanding that our books be read.

Am I talking about protection? Yes, I am. I do think that there is a role for government to play in defending cultural production in a nation. The belief that creative arts need to be supported is incontestable in most of the civil democratic world. Our cousins in English—the Americans and the British—are countries that protect the territorial copyright and property rights of their publishers. Globalisation has been a liberalising force but within its market logic there is a prioritising of the immediate over the long term. We all know from our own love of reading, viewing, of listening, that it can take time for a work of art to find an audience; it can also take time before we understand what was truly potent or brave or inspiring about a book or a film or a musical composition. The loyalty and trust I have been referring to as central to the Australian book industry is expressed in a publisher's continual support of a writer who might not have produced a bestseller. That too is a form of protection and I would not have survived as a writer without it.

We writers, we artists, we want to see ourselves as existing in a world beyond borders. We are, for the most part, of the cosmopolitan class. In my support for the retention of PIRs am I arguing that the livelihood of a worker in publishing is qualitatively more important than that of a worker in the auto industry? That's an assertion I am loath to make and which I think is indefensible. I wish we had made terrific Australian cars. But we didn't and that, in part, was because of the short-sightedness of many of our politicians, economists and unionists. I do know, however, that we have produced great Australian books and we are continuing to produce great Australian books. I also know that there is a special excitement that comes from reading an Australian work that opens up our own world, our own history, our own culture to examination and insight. I have a special relationship with Australian literature that is vastly different from the one I have with that of any other country. I support the publishers in their unified resistance to the removal of PIRs because I am satisfied that they understand their roles as custodians of our art, of our culture.

Not everyone is going to agree with my argument, including some of my fellow writers. My sense is that as long as the economic liberal consensus holds, it will be an argument that we will keep returning to. In affirming my faith in the publishing world, which is really a trust in the people who work in it, I am not unaware that there are real concerns that need to be addressed. The argument against the price of books here is overstated and I have little patience with consumers who argue that they can get a book for $2.50 less on Amazon. If we are to support Australian writing, that also means supporting the booksellers in this country. Just as the publishers are advocates for our work, so are they. Every week in my inbox I receive notices from bookshops informing me of a brilliant new Australian title, or sending me an invitation to an author talk, an opportunity to engage with an author I admire. That doesn't happen on Amazon. Unfortunately, globalisation has trained us well and we too often clamour for the immediate over the sustainable.

Where I do think a change needs to occur is in the cost of textbooks in this country. I think it unconscionable that students have to pay such inflated prices for scholastic and academic texts. The crisis in education in this country is real, we all know it, and the increasing inequality of education is something that we as booklovers have to become bolder in decrying. This would be an area in which I would like the Productivity Commission to do further work and it is also one I would like publishers to address.

If publishers accept the role of custodianship I have been arguing for, then I also think they need to come to the table as a united body with concrete ideas for reinvigorating the publishing of poetry, of the essay and of the short story in Australia. In particular, the abandoning of poetry, one of the great literary forms and great achievements of the Australian literary canon, is a disgrace. I know there is a bottom line but the resistance to the abandoning of the PIRs is made in a language across our publishing world that says the word is more important than the dollar. I am asking the publishers to be true to that.

That behemoth the music industry has shrunk and withered and no-one mourns its passing. I came into adulthood at a wonderful time for Australian music, the era of The Birthday Party and The Go-Betweens, The Saints and Radio Birdman. Their music still reverberates and its echo can be heard in new work being created by suburban kids in garages across the world. But I also remember how hard it was for those bands to make a living, how it took a long time to become popular; and that it was a network of community radio, independent music shops and clubs, music writers and obsessed fans that were their true supporters. The music industry wasn't there for them, as the producer of their music, and that's why none of us give a fuck that it shattered. But that isn't what I have experienced as a writer dependent on the Australian publishing and bookselling industries. We writers aren't only supporting them out of self-interest. We want to return some of that faith and trust. The economists and politicians should come and talk to us, they should hear our stories.

Tim Winton

I'm surprised and very pleased to have this little book acknowledged by the industry in this way. So, thank you.

When I was writing this book I was never really sure what it was. Now that it's safely behind me, I see that *Island Home* is a kind of love letter—to this place, its ecosystems and creatures, but also to its people. As I say somewhere in the book, this country leans in on you, it weighs down hard. Like family. Because it *is* family. And whether I like it or not, I'm caught up in its web, ensnared in all those family matters, organic and intangible, functional and dysfunctional, many of which make me shout at the telly and howl at the moon.

All the same, I love this family. It's where I'm from and it's what formed me. And I want to defend it. I want to see it continue to mature and develop and prosper. I love its myriad stories, its particularities, its peculiar sounds. And that's not one monolithic story or voice, by the way. It's the voice of Steve Irwin, say, but also the voice of Lee Lin Chin; it's the sounds of Gurrumul *and* of Katie Noonan; the stories of Tom Keneally *and* of Alexis Wright.

Australia has survived its colonial era. It's too cute to say we've left it behind completely, but in my lifetime we've striven to out-think and outgrow it. We've begun to sing and dance and play and write and, yes, to legislate our way past a colonial existence. And our arts community has been integral to this change of mindset. Australian writers and publishers have been at the forefront of this evolution. Despite many cultural and geographical obstacles, we made ourselves up as we went along. We've done our own peculiar things and sent them out to the world beyond, honouring the specific and trusting in that enough to see it become universal. We've done this despite the headwinds of world publishing. Because as you know, in publishing terms, imperial power still resides in New York and London. And of course, in Gütersloh in Germany.

Books like *Possum Magic, The Book Thief, The Narrow Road to the Deep North, The True History of the Kelly Gang, The Slap, The Secret River*—all these were the fruits of a publishing culture that allowed its writers to speak to their own, a culture that nurtured these writers long enough for them to break out. And, of course, to publish—from home to the world—on just and logical terms.

So it distresses me to see how anxious our technocrats are to piss all this work up against the wall.

Part of what makes our industry viable and our literary output distinct is the concept of territorial copyright. And once again it's under threat. Not in New York or London of course. The Americans and the Brits aren't stupid; they'll keep theirs because to give that up is to set fire to your own house.

No, sadly, it'll only be us doing that. We'll be the ones putting ourselves at a self-destructive disadvantage. To no logical purpose whatsoever.

This pointless abrogation of independence will usher in a new colonial era of publishing. Once again Australian writers will be edited in London and read in export editions as they were when I was a kid. That's a huge and pointless step backwards. Back to tugging our forelocks like good colonial subjects. Or just giving in and getting on the boat.

Australian culture is the product of a fractious family, it's true, but we're a proud and passionate mob all the same. We still have a keen sense of fairness and loyalty and a good nose for bullshit. And we know there's no humiliation like that of the team that kicks an own goal. There's no disgust, no self-hatred to rival that feeling.

And yet this is what the Turnbull Government is flirting with. A massive own goal. And I don't know about you, but I can't believe we'll put the fate of our culture in the hands of a few wonks and technocrats who won't be here in ten or twenty years to pick up the pieces.

This isn't about book prices. Nor is it about the seamless flow of information. And it's certainly not about free and fair trade. It's about a mindset that thinks every wrinkle needs an iron, every nail a hammer, and every hill a bulldozer. It's about *ideology*, the beige business model that reduces every human endeavour to monoculture. It's about assuming a culture's intangible complexities can be read exclusively and competently through the blinkers of supply-side economics.

Australians are a hardy lot, but they're not masochists. And they don't like being taken for fools. They're also passionate and loyal readers. And once they get past the wonkery that's been dished up they'll see what's about to be taken from them. Their own voices, their unique sound, their irreplaceable stories. And I reckon they'll be pissed off.

There's an election in July. Australian readers need good, clear information about what's at stake. It's the job of the Australian publishing family to let them know. Right now.

A speech given at the Australian Book Industry Awards, Sydney, 17 May 2016

Contributors

Australian-born **Geraldine Brooks** is an author and journalist who grew up in Sydney's western suburbs. In 1982 she won a scholarship to the journalism master's program at Columbia University in New York. Later she worked for *The Wall Street Journal*, where she covered crises in the Middle East, Africa and the Balkans. In 2006 she was awarded the Pulitzer Prize in fiction for her novel *March*. Her novels *Caleb's Crossing* and *People of the Book* were both *New York Times* bestsellers, and *Year of Wonders* and *People of the Book* are international bestsellers, translated into more than twenty-five languages. She is also the author of the acclaimed non-fiction works *Nine Parts of Desire* and *Foreign Correspondence*. In 2011 she presented Australia's prestigious Boyer Lectures, later published as *The Idea of Home*. In 2016 she was appointed Officer in the Order of Australia for her services to literature. Her latest novel, *The Secret Chord*, was published in October 2015.

Geraldine Brooks lives in Massachusetts with her husband, author Tony Horwitz, and their two sons.

Isobelle Carmody is one of Australia's most highly acclaimed authors of fantasy. At fourteen, she began *Obernewtyn*, the first book in her much-loved Obernewtyn Chronicles, and has since written many works in this genre. Her novel *The Gathering* was joint winner of the 1993 Children's Literature Peace Prize and the 1994 CBCA Book of the Year Award, and *Greylands* was joint winner of the 1997 Aurealis Award for Excellence in Speculative Fiction (Young Adult category), and was named a White Raven at the 1998 Bologna Children's Book Fair.

Isobelle's work for younger readers includes her two series, The Legend of Little Fur, and The Kingdom of the Lost, the first book of which, *The Red Wind*, won the CBCA Book of the Year Award for Younger Readers in 2011. She has also written several picture books as well as collections of short stories for children, young adults and adults.

After living in Europe for more than a decade, these days Isobelle divides her time in Australia between her home on the Great Ocean Road in Victoria, and Brisbane, where she is working on a PhD at the University of Queensland. She lives with her partner and daughter, and a shadow-black cat called Mitya.

Peter FitzSimons is a journalist with *The Sydney Morning Herald* and *The Sun-Herald*. He is the author of over twenty-seven books—including biographies of Charles Kingsford Smith, Nancy Wake, Kim Beazley, Nene King, Nick Farr-Jones, Steve Waugh and John Eales—and is one of Australia's biggest-selling non-fiction authors of the last fifteen years.

Richard Flanagan was born in Longford, Tasmania, in 1961. His six novels are published in forty-two countries and have received numerous honours, including the 2014 Man Booker Prize for *The Narrow Road to the Deep North*. He is the Boisbouvier Chair of Australian Literature at Melbourne University.

Jackie French is an internationally award-winning writer and wombat negotiator, and was the Australian Children's Laureate for 2014–15 and the 2015 Senior Australian of the Year. In 2016 Jackie became a Member of the Order of Australia for her contribution to children's literature and her advocacy for youth literacy. She is regarded as one of Australia's most popular children's authors, and writes across all genres—from picture books, history, fantasy, ecology and sci-fi to her much-loved historical fiction. 'Share a Story' was the primary philosophy behind Jackie's 2-year term as laureate. You can visit Jackie's website at: www.jackiefrench.com.

Anna Funder's *Stasiland* was awarded the Samuel Johnson Prize. Her novel *All That I Am* won the Miles Franklin Literary Award, along with the West Australian Premier's Book Award, the West Australian Premier's People's Choice Award, the Barbara Jefferis Award, Indie Book of the Year, Indie Best Debut Fiction, the Australian Book Industry Award (ABIA) Book of the Year, ABIA Literary Fiction Book of the Year and the Nielsen BookData Bookseller's Choice Award. *All That I Am* spent over one and a half years on the bestseller list, several times at number one. Both books are published in twenty countries and translated into many languages. Anna lives in Sydney.

Nikki Gemmell is the bestselling author of thirteen novels and four works of non-fiction. Her books have been translated into twenty-two languages. She was born in Wollongong, New South Wales, and lived in London for many years, but has now returned to Australia. Her distinctive writing has gained her critical acclaim in France, where she's been described as a 'female Jack Kerouac'. The French literary magazine *Lire* has included her in a list of what it called the fifty most important writers in the world—those it believes will have a significant influence on the literature of the twenty-first century. Four books by Gemmell—*Shiver, Cleave, The Bride Stripped Bare* and *The Book of Rapture*—made the longlist of 'Favourite Australian Novels' as chosen by readers of the *Australian Book Review*. Nikki is currently a columnist for *The Weekend Australian*'s colour supplement magazine.

Morris Gleitzman is a bestselling Australian children's author. His books explore serious and sometimes confronting subjects in humorous and unexpected ways. His titles include *Two Weeks With the Queen, Grace, Doubting Thomas, Bumface, Give Peas A Chance, Extra Time, Loyal Creatures* and the series *Once, Then, Now, After* and *Soon*. Morris lives in Sydney and Brisbane, and his books are published in more than twenty countries.

Kate Grenville is one of Australia's most celebrated writers. Her bestselling novel *The Secret River* received the Commonwealth Writers' Prize, and was shortlisted for the Man Booker Prize and the Miles Franklin Literary Award. *The Idea of Perfection* won the Orange Prize. Grenville's other novels include *Sarah Thornhill, The Lieutenant, Lilian's Story, Dark Places* and *Joan Makes History*. Kate lives in Sydney and her most recent book is *One Life: My Mother's Story*.

Andy Griffiths is one of Australia's most popular children's authors. Andy is best known for The Treehouse series, the Just! books and *The Day My Bum Went Psycho*. Over the last twenty years Andy's books have been *New York Times* bestsellers, adapted for the stage and television and won more than fifty Australian children's choice awards. Andy, a passionate advocate for literacy, is an ambassador for The Indigenous Literacy Foundation and The Pyjama Foundation.

Andy Griffiths and Terry Denton began their creative partnership with *Just Tricking!* in 1997. They have now collaborated on eight Just! books (with more than a million copies sold), the groundbreaking *The Bad Book*, *The Cat on the Mat is Flat*, the bestselling *The Very Bad Book* and now the Treehouse series. Andy and Terry have won numerous kids' choice awards and many of their titles are nominated every year. *The 13-Storey Treehouse*, *The 26-Storey Treehouse*, *The 39-Storey Treehouse*, *The 52-Storey Treehouse* and *The 65-Storey Treehouse* have all won Australian Book Industry Awards.

Jane Harper has worked as a print journalist for thirteen years both in Australia and the United Kingdom, and now lives in Melbourne. Winner of the Victorian Premier's Literary Award for an Unpublished Manuscript, *The Dry* is her first novel, with rights sold to over twenty territories. In its first four weeks of publication, *The Dry* was the number one Australian fiction title.

Chloe Hooper's first novel, *A Child's Book of True Crime*, was shortlisted for the Orange Prize for Fiction and was a *New York Times* Notable Book. *The Tall Man*, her non-fiction account of the death in custody of Cameron Doomadgee, won many literary awards. Her most recent book *The Engagement* is a taut and provocative psychological thriller.

Toni Jordan is the author of four novels. The international best-seller *Addition* was a Richard and Judy Book Club pick and was longlisted for the Miles Franklin Literary Award. *Fall Girl* was published internationally and has been optioned for film, and *Nine Days* was awarded Best Fiction at the 2012 Indie Awards, was shortlisted for the Australian Book Industry Awards Best General Fiction award and was named in *Kirkus Review*'s Top 10 Historical Novels of 2013. Her latest novel is *Our Tiny, Useless Hearts*. Toni lives in Melbourne.

Thomas Keneally won the Booker Prize in 1982 with *Schindler's Ark*, later made into the Steven Spielberg Academy Award-winning film *Schindler's List*. His non-fiction includes the memoir *Searching for Schindler* and *Three Famines*, an *LA Times* Book of the Year, and the histories *The Commonwealth of Thieves*, *The Great Shame* and *American Scoundrel*. His fiction includes *Shame and the Captives*, *The Daughters of Mars*, *The Widow and Her Hero* (shortlisted for the Prime Minister's Literary Award), *An Angel in Australia* and *Bettany's Book*. His novels *The Chant of Jimmie Blacksmith*, *Gossip from the Forest* and *Confederates* were all shortlisted for the Booker Prize, while *Bring Larks and Heroes* and *Three Cheers for the Paraclete* won the Miles Franklin Literary Award. *The People's Train* was longlisted for the Miles Franklin Award and shortlisted for the Commonwealth Writers' Prize, South East Asia division. His most recent book is *Napoleon's Last Stand*, published by Random House.

David Malouf is the internationally acclaimed author of novels including *Ransom*, *The Great World* (winner of the Commonwealth Writers' Prize and the Prix Femina Étranger), *Remembering Babylon* (winner of the IMPAC Dublin Literary Award), *An Imaginary Life*, *Conversations at Curlow Creek*, *Dream Stuff*, *Every Move You Make* and his autobiographical classic *12 Edmondstone Street*. His *Collected Stories* won the 2008 Australia–Asia Literary Award. His most recent books are *A First Place* and *The Writing Life*. He was born in 1934 and was brought up in Brisbane.

One of the stars of Australian fiction, **Monica McInerney** is the author of the internationally bestselling novels *A Taste for It*, *Upside Down Inside Out*, *Spin the Bottle*, *The Alphabet Sisters*, *Family Baggage*, *Those Faraday Girls*, *At Home with the Templetons*, *Lola's Secret*, *The House of Memories* and a short story collection, *All Together Now*. *Those Faraday Girls* was the winner of the General Fiction Book of the Year prize at the 2008 Australian Book Industry Awards. In 2006 Monica was the ambassador for the Australian Government initiative Books Alive, with her novella *Odd One Out*. Monica grew up in a family of seven children in the Clare Valley of South Australia and has been living between Australia and Ireland for twenty years. She and her Irish husband currently live in Dublin.

Alex Miller's novels have all been critically acclaimed and have won or been shortlisted in the major Australian literary awards. He is twice winner of Australia's premier literary prize, the Miles Franklin Literary Award, and is an overall winner of the Commonwealth Writers' Prize for *The Ancestor Game*. His eleventh novel, *Coal Creek*, won the 2014 Victorian Premier's Literary Award. Miller's most recent work, *The Simplest Words*, is his first collection of stories, memoir, commentary and poetry.

Alex Miller is published internationally and his works have been widely translated.

Frank Moorhouse has written seventeen books, mainly novels, published over a hundred short stories, and as many essays. All his books have been constantly in print. He has won major national prizes in each of these forms. Last year he was made a Doctor of Letters (*honoris causa*) by the University of Sydney. He has no assets (except for his copyrights) and over the years has often been broke. He is not whingeing but says he is urging.

Matthew Reilly is the international bestselling author of the Scarecrow novels: *Ice Station*, *Area 7*, *Scarecrow*, *Scarecrow and the Army of Thieves* and the novella *Hell Island*; the Jack West novels: *Seven Ancient Wonders*, *The Six Sacred Stones* and *The Five Greatest Warriors*; the standalone novels: *Contest*, *Temple*,

Hover Car Racer, *The Tournament*, *The Great Zoo of China* and *Troll Mountain*. His next novel to be published in 2016 has Jack West Jr return in *The Four Legendary Kingdoms*.

His books are published in over twenty languages, with worldwide sales exceeding seven million copies.

In 2011 *Scarecrow and the Army of Thieves* was the biggest-selling fiction title released in Australia for that year. Three more of Matthew's books have been the biggest-selling Australian fiction titles of their year of release: *The Tournament* (2013), *Seven Ancient Wonders* (2005) and *The Five Greatest Warriors* (2009).

Before becoming a novelist, **Michael Robotham** was an investigative journalist working across Britain, Australia and America. He is the author of twelve *Sunday Times* bestsellers, both fiction and non-fiction. He has also worked as a ghost-writer for prominent military figures and star performers, as well as in the fields of science, sport and psychology.

Michael's haunting psychological thrillers have been translated into twenty-three languages and are currently in development for TV by Bonafide Films. He is a two-time winner of the Ned Kelly Award for Australia's Crime Novel of the Year. He has twice been shortlisted for The Crime Writers' Association (CWA) Steel Dagger and won the prestigious CWA Gold Dagger Award in 2015 for *Life or Death*. His latest novel, *Close Your Eyes*, was published in August 2015.

Magda Szubanski is one of Australia's best known and most loved performers. She began her career in university revues, then appeared in a number of sketch comedy shows before creating the iconic character of Sharon Strzelecki in ABC-TV's *Kath and Kim*. She has also acted in films and stage shows. Her first book, *Reckoning: A Memoir*, won Book of the Year and Biography of the Year at the 2016 Australian Book Industry

Awards, and was awarded the Douglas Stewart Prize for Non-Fiction in the NSW Premier's Literary Awards, the Indie Award for Non-Fiction, and the Nielsen Bookdata Booksellers' Choice Award. Magda lives in Melbourne.

Christos Tsiolkas is the author of five novels: *Loaded*, which was made into the feature film *Head On*, *The Jesus Man* and *Dead Europe*, which won the 2006 *Age* Fiction Prize and the 2006 Melbourne Best Writing Award. His international bestseller, the acclaimed novel *The Slap* won Overall Best Book in the Commonwealth Writers' Prize 2009 and the Australian Literature Society Gold Medal; was shortlisted for the 2009 Miles Franklin Literary Award, longlisted for the 2010 Man Booker Prize, and was also announced as the 2009 Australian Booksellers Association Book of the Year and Australian Book Industry Awards Book of the Year. Christos' fifth novel, *Barracuda*, was published here and in the United Kingdom to rave reviews in late 2013 and became an instant bestseller. The ABC drama series of *Barracuda* aired in July 2016. Christos' latest book is *Merciless Gods*, a short fiction collection which won the 2015 Steele Rudd Award. Christos is also a playwright, essayist and screenwriter. He lives in Melbourne.

Tim Winton is one of Australia's most acclaimed writers, thinkers and essayists. He is the author of twenty-eight books and three plays. His non-fiction has appeared in *The New York Times*, *Granta*, *The Monthy*, *The New Statesman*, *Prospect*, *The Los Angeles Times*, *The London Review of Books* and *The Economist/ Intelligent Life*. Since his first novel, *An Open Swimmer*, won the Australian Vogel Award in 1981, he has won the Miles Franklin Literary Award four times (for *Shallows*, *Cloudstreet*, *Dirt Music* and *Breath*) and has twice been shortlisted for the Booker Prize (for *The Riders* and *Dirt Music*). He lives in Western Australia.

If you would like to join the copyRIGHT fight and save our Australian stories here are two things you can do immediately:

---

1. Sign the petition
   www.change.org/p/scott-morrison-save-australian-literature-stop-parallel-importation-of-books.

We need all the signatures we can get to make our voice heard by government. Tell your friends about it.

2. Get involved in the Books Create campaign:

HERE ARE ALL THE RELEVANT DETAILS
Website: www.bookscreateaustralia.com.au

🐦 @bookscreateaus 📷 @bookscreateaus f facebook.com/Bookscreate

Hashtags: #bookscreate #copyrightmatters #OzBooks

Follow Books Create on these platforms and share, comment, like, favourite and retweet. Any action that you take will help amplify the message and push it out to your followers/friends.

You can combine the #bookscreate hashtag with other words: #bookscreate movies / #bookscreate empathy / #bookscreate jobs etc.

The key is to get involved in any way that you can.